Transplanted Heads

Your Muse Can't Write Worth Sh*t
a sequel to **How to Write a Book: Park It, Get to Work**

Sherrill Wark

A Crowe Creations Publication
crowecreations.ca

First publication © 2015 WordPress as sherrillwark.com
First Crowe Creations Edition, January 2020 © Sherrill Wark

All rights reserved.

Cover photo © iStock by Getty Images
Cover design © 2020 Crowe Creations

Interior design © Crowe Creations
Interior text set in Times Roman
Headings set in Zolano Serif BTN

Crowe Creations
ISBN: 978-1-927058-63-3

Dedicated to my very first Muse: Daddy.

"The best thing about being a writer is you can kill off your enemies without going to Court over it." — Christina Crowe

Foreword

*Transplanted Heads: Your Muse Can't Write Worth Sh*t* was once a WordPress blog. Up there for all to see. You could have read this for free back in 2015–16. I produced posts for a whole year. I have translated it into print but I'm not going to apologize for all the bolded words and underlines in its [genetically modified] print clone, because I am always trying to Break My Programming. (You'll have to read *How to Write a Book: Park it, Get to Work** to know what breaking one's programming is about.) Excerpts from *HtWaB* were included in the blog so they're in this project, too. I figured there was no point in re-writing something I had already written and which would probably come out sounding the same anyway. There aren't many but they fit. I also decided to keep the colour even though the price of this book would skyrocket. And since I'm not an artist, I purchased the rights to use graphics (credentials are in Appendix 1) that suited the subject of the posts rather than pay thousands of dollars to have a single artist try to draw the pictures in my right brain.† Purists will no doubt wrinkle their noses. Sorry.

    I don't think many read my blog. Some of my writerly friends Followed me. (Thank you.) I do have friends other than writers. Between you and me, I think our non-writerly friends are overly humble, so much so that they feel they couldn't possibly be good friends with A Great Writer so they aren't going to go out and buy a book in case we ask them how they liked it and they didn't. But that's OK, too. I often hear people describe their disappointment with the writing world, that they are "not getting anywhere" with their writing. One of my colleagues seems to get the most downhearted just before publishing day and says, "Yeah. All ten of my fans are going to rush right out there and buy it, aren't they?" Another says, "I am getting discouraged with this writing business. I thought I could make a living with it." This is something I find difficult to understand and it's mutual because they do not understand that I have this passion (disorder?) to write. Just to write. Not to sell. Just write. I've always loved writing. When my father was away at police school — I don't think they called it police academy back in the '40s (that would be the **19**40s) — I remember being frustrated that I couldn't write him a letter back because I didn't know how to write. I would have been around five years old, so pre-school. We were "monetarily disadvantaged" in those days (and the children's section of the Perth, Ontario, library was quickly depleted), so Dad made up bedtime stories for me and encouraged me to tell him stories back. Essentially, I've been "writing" for about seventy years. And I don't plan to stop. And I write for no other reason than to write.

SW
2020

---

*HtWaB was previously published as *Really Stupid Writing Mistakes: How to Avoid Them*. Although my writing colleagues — those who know me well — absolutely loved the title, the marketing expert I hired [https://sarahsambles.com/blog/], told me to ditch the title and especially the cover, and redo it. I did. I think I sold three copies, two of them accidentally to loyal writer friends who thought it was my latest book. Sorry.
"†I once asked my kid sister, back when we were learning how to be psychic Hippies, if she wanted to take a look at my mind. She said, "***GOD, NO!***"

Table of Contents

Muse? What's a Muse?	1
The Importance of Keeping Secrets	2
I Don't Know How to Start	4
Naming Our Characters: Part 1	7
Naming Our Characters: Part 2	9
Naming Our Characters: Part 3	11
Let's Get Started	13
Genre = Species	15
Story Structure	17
Surprise! Surprise!	19
Leaving Bread Crumbs	21
No Loose Threads	23
Develop Laryngitis — Use the Right Voice	25
Don't Stalk Your Characters	27
Dialogue Maketh the Character	30
The TV Brain = Talking Heads	33
How to Get Away With Switching POVs	35
Subtext — Talkin' Dirty	37
Making a Character Loveable	40
Making a Character Killable	42
Make 'em Wanna — Motivation	44
Conflict is Required	46
Dilemma = Motivation = Story!	48

Go Ahead — Manipulate Your Readers	50
Be Kind to Your Critters	52
Yes, We Can Be Too Nice	54
An Opinion for EVERY Character	56
Don't Muzzle Your Characters	58
Using Backstory without Using It	61
Describe without Details	64
Describe through Action	67
Blame it on Writer's Block	69
Two Books in One?	71
Not Enough Novel for a Novel?	73
Too Many Cooks	75
Recycling Characters	77
Making Your Grammar App Weep	79
The Mysterious Comma	81
Remain In-Tense — Verbs 1	84
Remain In-Tense — Verbs 2	88
Oops! Dammit! & Other Exclamations	91
Malapropisms — Say it Isn't So	95
Author Intrusion & Other Writing Crimes	98
My Boss Is a Tyrant 1	100
My Boss Is a Tyrant 2	102
My Boss Is a Tyrant 3	105
De-Stressing	107
I Don't Know How to Finish	111
Indie Publishing	113
Do-It-Yourself Publishing	115
Taming the e-Monster	117
When Do My Millions Start Rolling In?	119
I'm Ready for my Close-Up, Mr DeMille	121
"The Last Post"	123
About the Author	125
Appendix 1: Photo/Graphics/Cartoon Credits by Chapter	127
Appendix 2: How to Disengage Microsoft Word's I'm-Only-Trying-to-Be-Helpful App	129
Appendix 3: Search/Replace	133
Appendix 4: Styles! The Most Amazing Assistant Ever!	136

Muse? What's a Muse?

I started writing poetry seriously back in high school and I even managed to get published. I believed from the bottom of my heart, that every word that came through my fingers onto the page — we used a thing called a "pen" and wrote on stuff called "paper" back then — was sacrosanct, from the gods, could not be altered without bringing onto oneself some strange curse that would alter our lives forever.

Some of us still believe that. (Me, for one, about my poetry until fairly recently.) We must throw that notion away right now! Not the idea of the Muse, but the idea that this Muse of ours funnels information to us with perfect grammar, spelling and syntax. Our ideas come from what we might *call* "Our Muse" but what is actually the concept side of our brain that can't spell cat without referring to our on-board dictionary (which probably has quite a bit of faulty information in it) on the opposite side.

That's why editors (like I used to be in another life) were invented. We can hand an editor an early draft — I am trusting it would *never* be a first draft. Nobody would, like, *ever* do *that*, would they? No, of course not. Then Mr. or Ms. Editor will give us an estimate based on the amount of work that's involved. The earlier the draft, the more work is involved in "fixing" it and the higher the cost will be to have it edited.

This editing cost can be as high as $5 a page just to fix the grammar, syntax and spelling, and nothing else. Multiply that by 300 pages and we're looking at a $1500 charge and our book can still be as boring as tapioca without the sugar and vanilla.

Several more sweeps through our own manuscripts with both eyes open to catch these easy-to-remove errors would be saving ourselves a lot of money up front. Not to mention embarrassment.

Future chapters will be addressing such errors and as we move along, we will get deeper into writing good story, too. Our stories are usually excellent (if we've been avid readers throughout our lives and know what's out there so we don't repeat and repeat), but if our stories are hidden within the brambles of bad grammar and spellos and commas— Oh, don't get me started on commas! That will be a whole entry on its own.

The Importance of Keeping Secrets

It's difficult enough to write a book without your mom — or your kids, these days — looking over your shoulder pointing out every little error in every little sentence as you go along. The moms usually add things like: "Oh b't you can't say THAT about HIM," or in my own case "Why don't you write something nice, dear?"

It's enough to make you go play Solitaire instead.

Rule #1

Don't ever, ever write for anybody else but yourself. This means you need to pretend that nobody will ever see it.

One way to get around this is to use a pseudonym but don't worry about all this just yet. You haven't even written it and you're already worried about what folks might say about it?

Actually, this is a good attitude to have (in a way). It means you believe that this book of yours will eventually be published. Good. Want it? Dream it. But until then, do not let anybody who knows you (friends, family, coworkers) see it. Don't let them see it until the book comes out. They can be the first to purchase copies. Yes?

The thing is, if you write well, if you capture humanity in its truest form — which is what a good writer does — every reader will recognize himself in at least one of your characters. And human nature will have him identifying with the worst of them. Uncle Charlie will be certain (as will Mom) that you wrote about him; your sister will call you a bitch for letting the world know about that night after the prom; or your wife will stop speaking to you.

Best to have the book finished, edited, published before they get started. Otherwise, you'll never get past the first chapter.

Rule #2

Just write. Don't worry about the correct word, about where those damnable quotation marks go (Canadians have this issue to deal with), about what you learned in school — *especially* what you learned in school, unless your teacher was Stephen King (or similar). Stephen King was a high school English teacher before he burst onto the scene with *Carrie*. Did you know that? Stephen King knows the rules of grammar.

Obviously, there's more to writing a book than knowing the difference between a gerund and an elbow, but it helps at that most-important edit stage. Which happens *after* you finish writing your book. Later. Write now, worry later.

Please note: No matter how long it takes you to finish that book, it's still a "first draft" so you might as well power through it and get the sucker done and deal with the elbows later.

So why does grammar and correct spelling and all that boring stuff that nobody cares about anymore matter so much? I'll write about this in another chapter.

Meanwhile, hunch over and vomit your guts onto the keyboard. Your Muse will urge you on but don't trust her with the spelling or word choices. (She has an awful habit of using malapropisms.)

I Don't Know How to Start

I was looking after the book table at a colleague's launch last year when a woman approached me and very quietly told me: "I want to write a book but I can't seem to get started. How do you start?"

I asked: "Do you know what it's about?"

"Yes."

"Do you know who's in it?"

"Pretty much. Yes."

"And you're having trouble starting it."

A nod.

"Do you know how it ends?"

She brightened up. "Yes! Of course I do." A shy laugh.

"Then start at the end and write backwards."

Nothing about How to Write Is Etched in Stone

There's more than one way to write a book. Women tend to think linearly and men in the big picture. "Tend to," I said. "Tend to."

If we find ourselves using either one of these thought patterns exclusively, it's time to … Ready, Class? It's time to ... Drum roll … <u>Break Our Programming</u> and do things in the opposite (or at least different) way.

Instead of writing the story as:

1. Mary's husband dies.

2. Mary now lives alone and doesn't like living alone.
3. Her children worry about her mental condition.
4. On the advice of her psychologist/priest/rabbi, Mary decides to travel to the coast to do some painting.
5. Mary meets John.
6. She thinks he's hot.
7. He stares back at her with desire.
8. She discovers something that makes him look like a bad guy.
9. They have a fight.
10. She finds out he isn't a bad guy, it's his evil twin that's the bad guy.
11. They make up.
12. They have sex.
13. They ride off into the sunset together to live happily ever after.

… We can change the order around and write it in random chunks to be fit together later — after the stress of getting the damned thing out of us is over and done with. Example, we can write the sex scene first, or the fight, or the discovery of the evil twin.

Or we can lay out a skeleton (the big picture) and fill in the muscle, bone and sinew from head to toe.

The main thing is, one doesn't need to write a book from beginning to end. Very often, the first couple of chapters should be tossed anyway.

But Backwards?

I'm always referring to books on screenwriting as being valuable. Writing backwards is something I learned from one of them. What are the advantages to writing a story backwards?

- Because of this, this happened and because of that, that happened, and because of this other thing and that other thing, these events happened.
- No effect without a cause. Tight writing.
- No loose threads. Everything ties in together eventually. No scattered bread crumbs. No subplot left unresolved. Neat and tidy and boxed up with paper and a bow.

The first time I tried writing a piece this way I snickered each time I threw in my foreshadowing. It was great. *Heh, heh. They will never know this is a foreshadow to that which is a foreshadow to this until she finds the key to the mysterious room at the end. Heh, heh.*

Working backwards I would have Mary find the second key — the one to the mysterious room (and what the story is all about!) — in the desk drawer.

1. Because she has opened the desk drawer with the first key.
2. Because she has found the first key on the top shelf of the library above the Arthur Conan Doyle books.
3. Because she has seen the butler's wife put something on that top shelf.

4. Because she has followed the butler's wife after she heard the woman and the footman whispering suspiciously out in the stables.

5. Because a nosy neighbour alerted Mary that something was going on between these two.

Why would the neighbour share that with Mary? She doesn't even know her. Or perhaps she does ... Did the neighbour and the footman have a falling out? Why was that?

Backwards? Why not?

Naming Our Characters: Part 1

Naming our people is a lot more difficult than we think. Especially if we've already written the book and have to go back and change those we love so very deeply into some unknown entity.

"But, but, but …"

I know, I know. There, there.

Hindsight makes us use bad words and get frustrated but we are doing this for the good of the book. Our readers won't know we've changed the names. Our characters won't even notice. Our characters are much more malleable/accepting about these things than we are.

However, if you need to go in there and change a name, this is how I do it.

Let's say we have discovered that we have a Fanny, a Fran, and a Frank in our book. (I'll explain later on why similar names, and even names with the same starting letter, are not a good idea.)

Let's say that Fran and Frank are minor characters and Fanny is important. Let's keep "Fanny" then. (If you don't already know how, see Appendix 3 for how to do a Search and Replace.)

Do a <u>Search</u> for the name Fran and <u>Replace All</u> with Felicity.

There we go. That was easy.

Oops.

What the heck is this word? Felicitytic. And what's this? Felicitytically, and this Felicityk, and this Felicityce?

Seems it found every single "fran" and changed it to Felicity: <u>fran</u>tic, <u>fran</u>tically, <u>Fran</u>k, <u>Fran</u>ce.

Poo.

Click Undo. (Two ways of doing that: (1) Click Edit up above on the left there and you'll see the Undo feature; or (2) Just click on the counterclockwise curly arrow up above there.) Click undo. Start over.

Find and replace all Frank with Ernest, first. Unless we've used "frankly, my dear" in our book, there shouldn't be too many other "franks" inside a word, although there are: frankfurter, Frankenstein, frankincense, Franklin, frankness, Frankfort, franks, Franktown, Frankton …

The faster way is the Find and Replace <u>all</u>, but if we have used Franklin or Frankenstein extensively in our book, we can do a single Find Next and replace and search for Frank one at a time. (I explain this in Appendix 3.) When you find it, click Replace. Then click Find Next again. Replace. It's slower this way, but perhaps quicker in the long run if it means we don't have to read the whole book over again.

But that's the hard way. I wanted you to see the hard way so you'd understand the principle behind it.

Naming Our Characters: Part 2

Why isn't it a good idea to name characters with similar names like Fanny, Fran and Frank? (Or even with the same beginning letter?)

If you've ever tried to proofread your own work, you'll understand the concept behind why it's difficult — if not impossible — to do. It's because our minds are nice to us. Our minds like to help us swim across the sentence moat into the castle of imagination. Our minds want to help us "see" what it thinks we expect to be there, like "and" instead of "adn". *No, no, silly. Those aren't piranhas, those are goldfish. Keep swimming.*

That's why I always tell my clients, when their book is at the final stages of design, when they have to give it that final run-through, to read it backwards.

"What?!!" they e-mail back to me, and I don't need to see their faces to know their eyes are wide with disbelief and even horror. "But I can't read it like that!"

"Esattamente!" I tell them. "We don't *want* to 'read' it at this stage. We want to fool our minds into actually *seeing* each word individually rather than assuming what might be there."

I soon get the next e-mail: "I caught a big one! And it was a whopper!"

It's a lot of work doing it that way, tedious, tiring, slow going but it's amazing how the errors seem to leap off the page.

When we read a novel, we like to get right into it. We like to imagine ourselves in the world the author has created for us and this to the point where we no longer even want to know that some author has created this world we are now exploring, living in. (When we get to this stage in our writing career, when we can cause our readers to want to shut us out, too, we've made it. We have arrived.)

When reading a well-constructed novel, we are in that delicate world between right and left brain, balanced on the rim of concept and detail, so every time we run across anything that tips us too far to one side, we fall into either the complete concept pool (where words do not exist, only pictures) or into the complete detail pool that has all the words and numbers and previously filed pictures (sort of) in it, but no imagination.

When we read about a character — for instance Fanny — we take a picture of that name and store it in our concept side. We merely need to see the capital letter "F" and perhaps the roundish letter "a", the smoothness of the "n", and we know this mental picture means our heroine, the girl/woman we're already deeply interested in and know a lot about.

On we read to possibly skim right over "Fran" the first time, or even the second. This will go on until we read something quite un-Fanny about what our minds had assumed *was* Fanny. *What's she doing with Joe? I thought she was married to Peter. What? SPLASH!* Into the detail side of our brain we go and out of the world we've been inside.

We might even have to go back and re-read several pages to figure out who the hell is who anymore. Annoyed, do we set the book aside?

Let's make a solemn vow right this instant never to push readers off that tenuous rim and in with the piranhas. Or the goldfish. Moats have neither. Trolls, drowned knights, swords, and the odd maiden perhaps — but that's another chapter.

Naming Our Characters: Part 3

Giving our characters suitable names is of utmost importance. Can you imagine Count Dracula with any other name? Scarlett O'Hara?

Excerpt from *How to Write a Book: Park it, Get to Work*

How perfect are the names Rhett Butler, J. Alfred Prufrock, Jane Eyre? Cat Ballou? Hannibal Lecter?

Back to the Internet again. It's possible to search for:

most popular boy name [year]

most popular girl name [year]

You can search for individual years and also for decades and eras.

names + 1950s

Or:

names 1950s

For computer newbies, change how you word your questions/phrases if you are having trouble finding the right information. But the more detail you use in your search string, the fewer hits you'll get. Also notice that I have not said "boy's name" with the apostrophe s. What the search engine looks for is the stem of the word, not its meaning. There's no need to capitalize any words, either.

[...]

Avoid names ending with s, like Charles, Hobbs, James, Ulysses, or Frances. And yes, all these names require the 's possessive — Jesus does not, nor does the historical Ulysses, but an Hispanic character named Jesús would need it. Please have pity on anybody who might be reading your work out loud if they have to refer to a modern Ulysses's oasis. And what about anyone wishing to visit the modern Ulysseses' family home? Save yourself grief and don't have any of your characters using names ending in s — first, or last.

[...] pay attention to what you're calling your guys and gals at the very outset. Once you've gotten to know and love (or hate) your people, it's a heart-breaking task to change their names later on. Avoid that mistake in the first place so it won't feel like you're saying goodbye to anyone you've gotten attached to.

Name-your-baby books which give historical and ethnic origins for names are an excellent resource. I once made the mistake of giving a Hindu character a Muslim first name and will be forever grateful to the person who pointed it out to me before I published it.

End of Excerpt.

Yes, some of this is similar information to earlier chapters but, as writing colleague and good friend, Sharyn Heagle, author of *A Clear Range of Vision,* often says: "Writers don't read." So consider what I've repeated as a slap upside the head and forgive me for it.

The lists of names you will discover almost always provide meanings for the names. Take advantage of this and use them for your good guys and bad guys. Perhaps give your antagonist (bad guy) the least popular name for the year he was born.

One last note about names, and I don't think I need to explain why: Don't use the name of someone close to you. A future chapter will go more deeply into using a friend or relative in your fiction in the first place.

HE'S VERY DISCIPLINED ABOUT HIS WRITING, THREE HOURS STARING AT A BLANK SCREEN EVERY MORNING AND FIVE IN THE AFTERNOON

Let's Get Started

Excerpt from *How to Write a Book: Park it, Get to Work*

Blank page. Blinking cursor . . . Now what?

As an illustration, I'll use one of my own genres, horror. In a way, the horror genre is an easy one to work with, but in another way, it's extremely difficult because everything's already been done to death — there are only so many monsters, only so many ways you can kill somebody.

When I speak of horror, I refer to thrillers, suspense movies, monster movies and books, ghosts, vampires, werewolves, big bugs, small bugs, germs, ghosts, magic, mutants, future worlds, past worlds, bogeymen, alien planets, space creatures, pandemics, semi-heroes, and quasi-villains.

I'm not a fan of slasher movies because if I want to see something *that* real life, I'll watch a certain TV channel's news broadcast. When I read a book or see a movie, I want to be transported into someone else's made-up world that I can escape from — if I want — by either closing the book, clicking the remote, or walking out of the theatre.

The horror genre works like this:

- pick a current fear of the day (1980s it was AIDS);
- design a monster to best illustrate that fear (an *Alien* which, "undetected, gestates inside a human body");

- develop some good-guy characters and some bad-guy characters (you'll also need a few stereotypes for early disposal and to set the mood);
- stick them all together in a place they can't get away from easily (on a rickety space ship Out There);
- let your characters figure a way out of it while the bad guys (opportunists looking for the ultimate weapon) oppose them at every turn; and
- then kill off the monster at the end.

There's your book/movie with (usually) a wonderfully cathartic ending. (*Alien* spawned three sequels.)

Disguise Your Monster

Unless you're writing for any religious publications which want the lessons to be totally transparent in order to parallel sacred writings, it's best to disguise your issue/nugget/monster no matter what the genre. Readers, particularly children, don't want anything fed to them. A story has more effect if we've had to figure out something on our own.

So pick a fear, a joy, a current issue, a current trend — whatever you want — and symbolize it. There's the basis of your story.

Drop in Your People

Once you figure out what annoys, scares, disgusts, angers, or what might drive your character over the edge of sanity, then design a building, town, village, city, undersea world, planet, universe, or anything else that will challenge your character's patience and/or safety the most, then ship, taxi, drive, beam up, fly, or otherwise transport him/her to where the worst possible situation for him/her is unfolding.

End of Except.

Genre = Species

The Importance — or Not — of Sticking to a Specific Genre

Sticking to one genre is particularly important if we are approaching traditional publishers. That's the way they like it for marketing purposes and they are the boss. Because otherwise, they won't take on our book.

There are several schools of thought when indie-publishing through places like Smashwords, Kindle Direct Publishing (Amazon), etc., though:

- Stick to a single genre (both in writing the book and in labelling it).
- If the book is a romance/history or perhaps a romance/thriller, a thriller/comedy, a sci-fi with a strong horror element like *Alien*, then change the BISAC category back and forth between the two every few months or so.* (BISAC Category: "Book Industry Standards and Communications (BISAC) categories are used by the book-selling industry to help identify and group books by their subject matter.")
- It is sometimes to our advantage to be in a category with the fewest books so this means we can get creative — within the categorizations available, that is. But don't ever mislead.

This is an excellent guide to ... well, making a killing on Kindle: http://www.amazon.com/Killing-Without-Blogging-Facebook-Twitter/dp/0984916172 by Michael Alvear.

---

*The one genre whose label we can't switch back and forth with any other is pornography. It must always have its Explicit Content warning.

More about Genres

Definition of "genre": https://www.vocabulary.com/dictionary/genre

Writer's Digest link: http://www.writersdigest.com/qp7-migration-all-articles/qp7-migration-fiction/genre-definitions

Another extensive list: http://www.cuebon.com/ewriters/genres.html

Wikipedia's take with its usual series of links to links to links that drive historical novel writers like me to distraction. Decide you need to check out 17th century pigeons and end up reading about dinosaur egg fossils for the rest of the day. https://en.wikipedia.org/wiki/List_of_writing_genres

A paragraph or so's description of several genres: http://www.dummies.com/how-to/content/exploring-the-different-types-of-fiction.html

Story Structure

I attended a weekend writing retreat a few years ago in which the presenter, Barbara Kyle, author, story consultant, story editor, and speaker, emphasized the importance of story structure.

Most of us roll our eyes and turn down the volume when anyone talks about laying out a story in advance of writing it. Half the time we don't know *what* we'll be writing or even how the story will play out until we get there. Our characters have their own way of doing things thank you very much.

As the weekend retreat fleshed out with valuable information, Barbara began to write a plot skeleton on the whiteboard, one vertebra at a time.

Wait a minute. This is starting to look really, really familiar!

This was reminding me of all the screenwriting books I've read, re-read and nearly wore the pages of to death with my constant underlining and highlighting. Books that I constantly recommend that *novel* writers consume as well.

And there she was, writing an all-too-familiar screenwriting skeleton on the whiteboard while telling us how to use it in our novels.

What Does Movie Structure Have to Do with Novel Writing? Story!

Human nature expects the Hero's Journey in stories. Even if we have never heard as much as a fairy tale in our life, our DNA desires the Hero's Journey structure.

This link lays the Hero's Journey out well: http://www.thewritersjourney.com/hero's_journey.htm

Rather than go on and on repeating what I've read in several books, I'll cite the titles of my two favourites (once again):

1. Eric Edson's *The Story Solution: 23 Actions All Great Heroes Must Take*
2. James Scott Bell's *Revision & Self-Editing: Techniques for transforming your first draft into a finished novel*

If you want a literal page-by-page skeleton (for a 120-page screenplay), try

- Todd Klick's *Something Startling Happens: The 120 Story Beats Every Writer Needs to Know*

To my rebellious nature, this latter book is total overload, but nonetheless extremely valuable. And please don't blame me — blame him! — if, after you read this one, your friends won't go to movies with you anymore because you'll be: "Hey. Right on. Minute 17! That's exactly what's supposed to happen."

Surprise! Surprise!

In the old days of Saturday afternoon Western movies at the O'Brien Theatre in my home town of Renfrew, Ontario, the Cavalry would often arrive at the last moment to save the day.

de·us ex ma·chi·na (dāəs eks ˈmäkənə, ˌdāəs eks ˈmakənə/); *noun*

1. an unexpected power or event saving a seemingly hopeless situation, especially as a contrived plot device in a play or novel.

("We" don't do that in our writing, do we?)

There's nothing as wonderful as a surprise ending whether it's in a movie, a story, a book or a poem. They're titillating so we love them.

Responsibilities

As writers, we have a responsibility not to make a fool out of ourselves by hauling in the equivalent of the cavalry to solve a story problem. That's being just plain lazy.

Can you imagine how ripped-off you'd feel getting to the end of a crime novel to learn that Joe Blow was the murderer but he wasn't even mentioned in the whole book until the very last sentence?

Far, far worse than learning that **the butler did it**.

"However!" she said, raising her index finger ... The butler is so rarely used as the murderer anymore that it just might *be* a big surprise for our readers.

Clues

Call them what you will — clues, bread crumbs, foreshadowing, warnings, signals — they are vital to any genre's surprise ending.

So we set up clues all along the way right under our readers' noses but expect to surprise them? How does that work?

Let's say we scatter three (or more) clues along the way then choose the least expected. To be fair, we can't do this without setting all three of these clues up as "suspects".

These extra clues must fit the story and connect as well. No cheating! No throwing stuff in just for the hell of it.

Muse Help

This is where our wonderful Muses can help us out.

This is where we have the most **fun** as writers.

This is also why it's paramount for authors to read, read, read, read, read so we can eliminate what every other author has used as a clue. We'll end up with something original, a real surprise for our treasured readers.

Leaving Bread Crumbs

The other day, while working on **Refuge in l'Acadie** (the second book in my Kesk8a series), my Muse suggested an interesting twist. I said to myself (I think I even said it out loud!): "Ooh yes! Like. Like."

This meant I had to go back into the story and tuck a **bread crumb** in early and I did this with great delight.

(I thank the Goddess of Cyberspace for inspiring the computer. It makes it so much easier to add this bit in here and move this bit to there and remove this silly bit than it was in Ye Olde Days when we used electric typewriters — or Before the Dawn of Time when we used manual typewriters.)

Bread crumbs are the basis of **mystery stories**. Imagine how utterly useless and beyond boring a mystery story would be without clues or foreshadowing (http://www.vocabulary.com/dictionary/foreshadowing).

We can **ramp up *any* genre** with bread crumbs to improve *any* story immensely.

From *Revision & Self-Editing: Techniques for transforming your first draft into a finished novel* by James Scott Bell:

> *A good discipline is to write as much detail about the ending as you can before you get there. How exhaustively you do this will depend on what kind of writer you are, but one of the benefits of this practice is that you can "marble in" action in your story that pays off later. This will give readers the feeling that there's more going on beneath the surface — always a good thing.*

In one of the [many] screenwriting books I've read/studied — and I apologize profusely for not remembering which one — I gleaned the greatest advice about writing a movie and I utilize it for *anything* I write now: **Write your story/book/movie backwards.**

Why? Cause and effect. **Effect and cause.** This happened because this happened because this happened … Backwards.

Any time the prolific Stephen King is asked *Where do you get your story ideas from?* he replies: "I ask myself 'what if?'"

Asking ourselves *what if?* sets the stage for not only the consequences of that "if" but will make us ask: why did this happen in the first place?

Equally as uninteresting as a mystery without set-up is an event with consequences only

The eruption of a volcano with its subsequent panic of townsfolk running here and there and interacting and causing lovely, lovely **conflict** among themselves is exciting. Yes.

Even more thrilling to read/watch is a book/movie in which the Antagonist (Bad Guy) did something to **cause** the volcano to erupt.

What **caused** the Antagonist to do this? And **Might he do it again, somewhere else? Oh, no!** is the essence of that question.

Was he compelled?

Is he a brilliant scientist and the *actual* Antagonist has, perhaps, kidnapped the scientist's daughter?

And why would this *actual* Antagonist decide to force a scientist to blow up a volcano in the first place?

Back up, back up, back up

A favourite TV series for me was *Motive*. Opening scene: some action goes on. A close-up. Across the bottom of the screen: **THE VICTIM**. Another scene. A close-up. Across the bottom of the screen: **THE KILLER**. Then the story of why the killer did it begins to unravel. https://en.wikipedia.org/wiki/Motive_(TV_series)

To weave subplots into our stories and have everything tie up neatly at the end, we almost *have* to start at the end and place our bread crumbs as we make our way to the beginning. This way, we will have no bread crumb without a reason for it.

No Loose Threads

Bread crumbs. Loose threads. = Food? Clothing?

Food, water, shelter, clothing, "love": the **necessities of life**.

These necessities keep our story characters alive, too.

Not only must we weave threads of **stories** and **substories** throughout our works (generally, only **one** story per **short story** though), but we must clothe our characters as well with those threads of story and substory. (I'll cover more about *clothing* characters in the chapter: "An Opinion for EVERY Character".)

Threads are important. (But not in the way of what "threads" meant back in my Hippy days when clothes were called "threads": "Nice threads, man," usually spoken with a cool marijuana-seeped voice, buddy to buddy.) Don't go overboard with what characters are wearing unless it matters to the story or serves as a deeper description of Protagonist/Antagonist.

> *"Her breasts sipped her soup when she leaned forward in that low-cut dress and gave him an appetite for more than lunch."*

Clothing, feeding and sheltering our characters need not necessarily be covered in great detail, but showing that main characters wear clothing (or don't), eat and live somewhere — be it in a mansion, an apartment, or on the street, in a city or a town — **adds dimension to both character and story**. Aim for ensuring that these details add to plot and/or **atmosphere** simultaneously.

I'm speaking of the threads that weave the tapestry of the whole story: the main characters' stories, substories and backstories; supporting characters' idiosyncrasies, stories, substories and backstories **IF** required; and set-up, setting, atmosphere, backdrop, clues, romantic connections, conflicts, substory or backstory for these conflicts …

Any time we start a thread in our story, we *must* tie it up before the end. Never leave a reader hanging no matter how slight the mention might be. This doesn't mean that every single *character* needs a thread, it means that every character we give a story to, must be followed up.

Example:

> *As Freddy sneaked through the park's thick trees, he passed behind a young man and woman on a bench. He overheard the woman.*
>
> *"I'll never leave you, Johnny. No matter what Daddy says."*

If Freddy had passed by this young couple and had noted arms around each other, eyes locked with love, warmth exuding from their closeness, etc., they would have been mere backdrop, scene description, perhaps mood enhancement.

By having the young woman tell Johnny her thoughts and thus expose a conflict in their lives to Freddy, the reader is alerted to their dilemma. The reader will wonder: *Oh. A divergence from Freddy's plight. How interesting. I wonder what's going to happen to these lovely young people. Are they part of the story?*

We don't want this to happen.

Or do we?

Perhaps further along in Freddy's story he *could* hear a ruckus behind him and have him hear Daddy's voice either chastising or praising. End of brief story. But why put that in anyway if it has nothing to do with Freddy? A brief story like this is merely a bit of fluff on a sweater to be plucked off at editing time.

Unless!

If Freddy is sneaking through the trees in the park to escape his own lover's father, this adds to *Freddy's* story so is fine to include as it's always good to have comparisons going on.

Substory threads that tie together in a single connected conclusion at the end of a novel or movie delight me to no end. This technique always draws a gasp of awe from me no matter the genre.

In order to weave a tapestry, the weaver must first tie some knots. Working backwards from the end of a story and pulling threads along that connect to each bread crumb we have dropped earlier, makes for a tapestry with no holes in it. One we can proudly display on our wall and brag: "See how it all comes together in one big beautiful picture?"

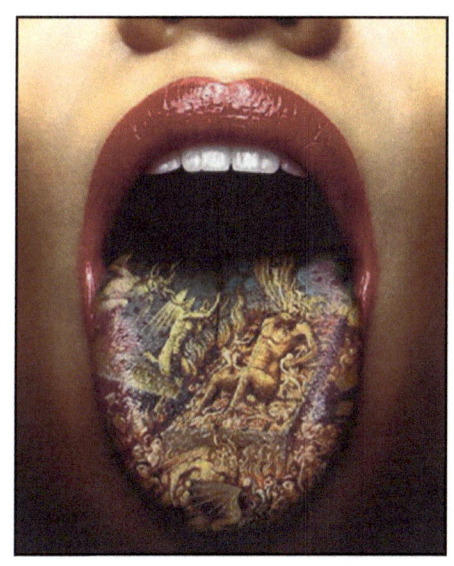

Develop Laryngitis — Use the Right Voice

Editing brings out the *narrator's* voice and suppresses our own. To make a beautiful garden, one has to trim branches and remove dried-up flowers. We become so used to hearing and saying phrases and words with friends and family, we don't notice the weeds sneaking up on us. Or the odd wildlife munching on the roses as they watch us through the window of our writing room. (Dare I say that something like the following can make it look like we were trying to reach a specific word count?)

We insult the reader's intelligence with:

- She had to make a decision ~~about what to do~~.
- She thought ~~to herself~~.
- She shrugged ~~her shoulders~~.

Leave Normal Everyday Stuff Out

"Hello," she said into her cell phone.
"Hello. Is this Mary?" asked John on the other end of the line.
"Yes, it is," she said.
"How are you?" he asked her.
"I am fine," said Mary. "How are you?" she asked.
"Fine. Do you want to go to the mall with me?" he asked.

"Yes. I would. What time will you be coming by to get me?" she asked.

This is an extreme exaggeration, but ...

Writing Like We Talk

This may sound contradictory, but if we think about it, our own regional accent is never the same as our narrator's voice. Our own regional accent is dialect. We must remove it from our writing. Unless, of course, we are writing in the 1st person and this <u>narrator</u> lives where we grew up so speaks the same dialect. But go easy with it.

For example: My mother grew up in RR 2, Tiny Village, Ottawa Valley, and any time I hear someone from that area talking, I know exactly where they grew up. It's a small, small pocket of Eastern Ontario with a unique voice.

"Hey. You're from Beachburg, aren't you?"

"Shurl! It's bin a dog's eej since we seen yer fizog."

Fizog?

[Pronounce the French word for face — *visage* — as an Anglo would and you'll get fizog. My grandfather used that all the time and I knew what he meant but not where it came from until well into my adulthood. I swear I laughed for a week when I figured out what it actually was. The Grant Settlement where he lived is right across the river from Quebec.]

If we are writing about characters living in another part of the country, or in another part of the world, we need to be wary of using regional terms familiar to us but not appropriate for the book we are writing.

If we are a British immigrant writing about a Toronto cop investigating a murder in Toronto, we can't have her drive to the suspect's house, park on the apron and open her boot. She would arrive at the suspect's house, park in the *driveway* and open her *trunk*. In Toronto. Or pretty much anywhere in Canada or the US. But if the narrator (you are the writer, not the narrator) grew up in England, then that's another story (pun intended) and we must write using *her* "voice" so *apron* and *boot* would be perfect.

Yes. Yes. Write what we know. But when we remove all our personal idiosyncrasies and regional syntax, what's left is the narrator's own unique voice. This is where we need to transplant heads. Not our head (regional accent) into the narrator's head, but his into ours so we can see his the way his is, not through the programming of our community, not through the (in my case, the Irish-influenced dialect of Renfrew, Ontario) green-tinted lenses of our own mind.

"But it doesn't sound like me anymore."

Good. It isn't supposed to. It's supposed to sound like the narrator. Nobody else. And this is yet another reason why reading, reading, reading every book we can get our hands and eyes on and into is a good idea.

Don't Stalk Your Characters

Let's ensure that our major characters live out their own lives while we **observe**, **read their minds**, and **record**.

However … we must not:
- follow their every single move;
- look in the mirror with them;
- go to the toilet with them (unless it's to see something unfortunate like blood in the urine or crabs in the pubic hair);
- go shopping with them — unless it's to purchase a gun, rat poison, the wrong flowers (or flowers on the wrong day). Not even Scrooge bought his own Christmas goose, he sent a minor character off screen to do it (and this added to **character** because he tipped the kid to do it).

Include only those activities that **advance the plot** and/or **show motivation** or **character**.

During my editing years, I often came across sections in manuscripts in which the authors couldn't seem to let their character go. (This usually happened at the end of chapters.)

In several ways, this delighted me. It meant that my constant harping about getting inside characters' heads, about transplanting their heads into our own, was paying off. The authors were falling in love with their characters. Wonderful. Absolutely wonderful.

Problems with including every action of a character:

1. when the action slows down that much, it leads the reader to expect something important is coming up;
2. it's fluff and we know it and when a reader realizes this as well, it turns them off;
3. since it usually happens at the end of a chapter/section, it blocks the opportunity (the ***required*** opportunity) to force the reader to turn the page; and
4. it almost always leads us away from the character's journey into our own journey which can be confusing to the reader: "I thought Suzie *liked* the smell of Parmesan cheese." And/or it may tempt us to throw in **the dreaded Author Intrusion**.

Example:

Marcie left the office and took the elevator down to the parking garage. She went to her car and started it. She left the garage and drove down Main Street and turned off at Bentley Avenue which was her street. At her house, she drove into the driveway, got out, locked the car and unlocked her front door and went in. She put her coat and things in the closet then went to the kitchen.

In the kitchen, she took out a pot and put it on the stove. From the cupboard, she took out a can of soup and with the can opener from the second drawer, she opened it and then put it into the pot. She turned on the stove.

After the soup was heated, she ate it from the pot with a spoon and then rinsed the pot in the sink and went to bed and fell asleep.

And, and, and? Then what happened? Was there a prowler? Did somebody break into her house? Did somebody put arsenic in the can of soup? Is she going to start throwing up? What's going to happen to Marcie?

Uh … nothing. That's just what she did after work. Every day after work except sometimes she heated a microwave meal … Every day. Day after day. The same thing that our readers do every day, too.

Let's not do this to our readers. Readers read books to escape from the mundane.

How about this?

Marcie was still steaming mad when she got home from work. There was no way Roger was going to get away with cheating on her. Not with that tart.

She threw her coat onto the chair at the front door and headed for the kitchen. He'd be home soon and she wanted to welcome him with an early supper. A special surprise.

She reached into the second drawer, took out the can opener. From the cupboard she took out Roger's favourite soup, Campbell's Chicken Noodle. Into a pot it went. Onto the stove it went.

From under the sink, way at the back, she took out the box of rat poison. ***END OF CHAPTER***

Otherwise, we don't need to know step-by-step details about our characters' actions.

Patricia K McCarthy Does it Well

(http://www.patriciakmccarthy.com/)

> *Patricia K. McCarthy is Ottawa's fang-queen, replete with sordid tales of horny vampires consorting with horny victims. Part blood bath and part bubble bath, her writing teases readers to make it to the end of each chapter alive. McCarthy was riding the vampire wave before there was one, which accounts for her biting flirtation with the dark art of satire. Read her Crimson vampire series and you may never feel the same again as you walk the streets of Ottawa when the sun goes down.* — Brant Scott, Capital Ideas Communication

In **Patricia K McCarthy's Crimson Series**, dear old Granny spends quite a lot of time in the kitchen where other characters often congregate. Granny doesn't always cook — most of the time she is doling out rum — but when she does cook, it's with lots and lots of background chatter **that advances the plot**. Always.

When we're in the kitchen with Patricia K McCarthy's Crimson Series characters, we know there is going to be a detailed change of plans.

When we're in the bedroom with her characters, the details are intimate.

When Magdalene is hungry, the details are delicious.

Although mentioned often, Granny's tomato soup cake recipe is not spelled out in the story itself. Ms. McCarthy provides the recipe at the end of Book 6, *The Crimson Dream* (*a vampire escape*), as a bonus for readers. Brilliant way of sharing a recipe with readers.

Or ...

Another way of handling a routine chore is to use it as **comedy relief** or perhaps **solve a problem** or take care of a **minor/major marital dispute** while simultaneously vacuuming or cooking (i.e., showing a character's skill set to make the reader "love" him/her).

> *No matter what Marcie did with her mother-in-law's apple pie recipe, it never came up to snuff according to her husband. She would change the type of apple she used, she would adjust the balance between white and brown sugar, she would adjust the amounts of cinnamon and nutmeg. Nothing worked. It was never the same as "Mom's" according to Roger.*

> *One day, Marcie got stuck talking to the neighbour out in the back yard while that week's apple pie was in the oven. It burned.*

> *You know what? she thought. I'm going to serve it to the son-of-a-bitch anyway. I'm sick and tired of his Mom-does-everything-better routine.*

> *That evening at supper she placed a piece of apple pie, edges blackened, crust dark brown, sugar hardened to amber, in front of Roger. As she turned to put the knife into the sink, she couldn't believe her ears:*

> *"You finally got it right, honey. It's perfect."*

Dialogue Maketh the Character

Excerpt from *How to Write a Book: Park it, Get to Work*

Are these examples true?

"Sufferin' succotash!" she mumbled.

"I don't give a damn," he hissed.

You can hiss "sufferin' succotash", but you can't mumble it and you can mumble "I don't give a damn", but you can't hiss it. The sentence has no sibilants.

If we are going to use attributives (she mumbled/he hissed, she said/he said) then we must ensure they match the dialogue. But if the dialogue itself indicates hissing or mumbling, then attributives become superfluous.

He started to stutter. "How . . . ? How . . . ?"

Stuttering *is* starting. Therefore, saying that a character started to stutter is redundant. Why do we need to tell our readers that he stuttered when the character's dialogue shows us? We're always being told "show don't tell," so we must remember that that carries into dialogue as well as into description.

Some how-to-write books tell us not to use attributives at all, even the he said/she saids. But then how are we ever going to show who's speaking? It's not as difficult as you might think: We get to know our characters intimately through questioning them, applying astrological traits (or whatever works for us) to them, and most important, we develop extensive back stories for them.

Let's have a look at a conversation involving three individuals:

(1)

"That's a nice bike."

"Thank you."

"I'd love to take it for a ride. May I?"

"Not without me."

"Let's go then. I'll just take it around the parking lot if you don't mind."

"Not without a license. Do you have one?"

"No, but I used to have one."

"You can't drive without a license."

"Yes, I can. Watch."

What do we know about these people from Conversation (1)? Nothing more than somebody-or-other has a nice bike and somebody-or-other else wants to drive it and you only know there's a third party in there because I told you. Everybody sounds exactly the same. In fact, they talk like the writer.

Now I'm going to tell you who the characters are: a Francophone biker chick, a Pentecostal minister's wife, and a veteran male police officer.

I'm going to change the vocabulary and the syntax. Let's see what we come up with.

(2)

"Afternoon, ma'am! Very nice ride you got yourself there."

"Why thank you, officer."

"Haven't been on an Indian for more years than I'd like to say. Think the Rev would let me take it for a spin?"

"As much I comply to nearly everything my husband tells me, I allow him no authority as to who rides my bike. You can certainly ride it. But not without me."

"Round the parking lot?"

"Hein, cochon! You got a license for dat?"

"Claudette! You're still driving that piece of shit Harley! I can't believe it. And since when did you ever worry about somebody breaking the law? Huh?"

"Go away from him, madame. He put my old man en prison. *He got no license. He can't drive that bike!"*

"You think ? Watch."

It's quite obvious who is speaking in Conversation (2) and not one attributive has been used.

You might be wondering why I had the police officer appear to know the woman's husband, therefore her, yet address her as "ma'am". If I hadn't told you he was a police officer, would you have been able to surmise it through his use of *ma'am*?

Try it yourself by switching to a male biker, a Roman Catholic nun, and a young female Francophone police officer. How about making up a scene using a fifteen-year-old girl from a disadvantaged family, the girl's mother, and our veteran male police officer?

Use a character's accent sparingly. The eye trips on misspelled words and having to deal with them throughout a whole book is tiring. To inform the reader that the speaker has an accent, first use a phrase in the speaker's language that might be easily understood by the reader, e.g., "*Hein, cochon!*" [Hey, pig!] (Foreign words and phrases which have not yet been accepted into English as standard are in italics. Or, since this entire passage is in italics, the foreign words, phrases, and any emphasized words are in roman.) Later, use expressions common in the speaker's language, but write them in English. If you listen to accents frequently — and I suggest you make a habit of it (check out news-talk radio stations) — you will detect a melody unique to each language and if you're at all musical, this should help you enormously. There is no need to misspell words at all, just play their tune the way they put their words together. It won't take long for the reader to accept the accent of the speaker.

End of Excerpt.

That being said about putting foreign phrases in italics, it depends. During my journeys through my Kesk8a series, I have played with that concept. Since Keskoua is telling her stories in English and quoting French and Mi'gmaw phrases — with which she is more than familiar — I am leaving them in roman. No italics. They are not foreign words to her, the narrator. I (she) use(s) italics only for phrases in languages unfamiliar to her: Portuguese, Dutch, Spanish, etc. But by Book 3, she is pretty good at some of those languages, too. In the words of a Francophone woman I used to work with when I was back typesetting: "H'it's depend."

The TV Brain = Talking Heads

Television shows are talk-talk-talk. Movies are walk-walk-walk. Books are neither. Books are both.

Books have the ability to get the reader right into the life of the character, "transplant" the reader's head into the mind, heart and soul of the protagonist (the hero/main character/whom the story is about) but sadly, fewer and fewer books are accomplishing this.

In order to have our readers experience the guts of the character, we as writers must be inside the head of that character, too, when we are writing. We can't jump over into Sally's head to see what she's thinking when we are inside what should actually feel like our own head (the current character) while we are writing. (This is called point of view, POV.)

Imagine being a plant. All your roots have little rootlets on them that tear off when you're pulled out of the ground. Imagine being uprooted, having your roots ripped up time and time again, every paragraph. *Ouch!*

We don't notice this in TV shows or in movies because these media are *visual* (and *aural*). The camera focuses on one character, then on another, then back again. Microphones pick up what the actors are *saying* to each other, not what the actors are *feeling*. A good actor will *show* you how the character is feeling but all this is against helpful background noises like sirens, soft music, creaking stairs, howling wolves ... to let us know further what the screenwriter wants us to experience. But we are still not inside the actual head/thinking process of any TV/movie character.

Any screenwriting coach will tell us: "You can't write *She is upset about her boyfriend's betrayal* because you cannot see that on screen. You need to write something like: 'Tears welling, Mary throws a flower vase at her boyfriend and rushes out of the room.'"

In books, we must do the opposite (but without writing *Mary feels)*.

For example:

That hurt. Mary had trusted him and he had spent the night with another woman. She dared not imagine his lips on that bitch's body. She wasn't about to risk prison by killing him but she certainly wanted to. She reached over for the flower vase. Right now, she could have crushed it in her hand but instead, she tossed it as hard as she could at those deceitful lips of his then hurried from the room, her face averted. She would not allow him to see the tears of frustration spill out of her eyes.

In soap operas, we follow several characters' stories simultaneously. In the soaps we know who is cheating on whom, who is lying, who secretly loves — or doesn't — another character.

Soaps are fun, full of intrigue and cheating spouses.

Movies are exciting, full of action.

Books need both but on a much deeper level. Why? Because they can.

Unfortunately, little by little, book writers are falling prey to following the camera around and *watching* their characters perform actions instead of climbing inside them and looking around from the inside where the character's thoughts and feelings reside.

Every time we rip our reader out of one character's brain and transplant him or her into another character's brain, we diminish our story a hundredfold if not more.

When we become adept at this concept of sticking with one POV only, our characters soar, our stories become riveting.

When our readers don't know what Handsome Stranger is thinking, they want to find out. It's human nature. Use it.

Make our readers crazy to know: Will Handsome Stranger fall in love with our protagonist? Or will he play her like her former boyfriend(s) did?

The moment we switch into Handsome Stranger's head with something along the lines of: *She is beautiful. I could certainly marry a woman like that ...* the tension for our readers disappears like children when it's time to do the dishes.

Tension creates excitement, worry, concern, stress, interest, a strong desire to continue reading, to turn the page.

How to Get Away With Switching POVs

Never ever change Point of View.

Except when …

I recently read Sonia Saikaley's novella, *The Lebanese Dishwasher*. [http://quattrobooks.ca/books/the-lebanese-dishwasher/] Although the same protagonist is used throughout the book, the book is written from both 1st Person and 3rd Person perspectives.

For the adult protagonist's POV, the story is written from the 1st person perspective. But the sections about Amir's past, his childhood, are written from the 3rd Person perspective.

Wait! Wait! Don't jump to any conclusions just yet. I did when reading it, but that lasted for only a sentence or two.

This is brilliant. Amir as a child experienced great pain — both emotional and physical — and this pain is so strong that psychologically, he has to set these experiences outside of himself, to think of himself as having been someone else when he went through these ordeals. Denial is neither stated nor implied but because Ms Saikaley chose to use 3rd Person for the child's section, this added an extra element, and it's a strong one. It "shows" how great Amir's denial is.

James Patterson changes POV to great effect in, e.g., *The Big Bad Wolf*, *Violets are Blue*, and *2nd Chance*, when he switches from good guy to bad guy. Being inside the head of the bad guy occasionally — in his own chapter — increases the tension, the suspense and the concern for the good guy because Patterson's bad guys are real sickos. Being inside the mind of a psychopath or a serial killer is quite scary if you imagine they are thinking about YOU (the reader) as their next project.

And how can I not mention that brilliant storyteller, Stephen King?

In *The Stand*, multiple protagonists scurry from various points in the USA, gathering fellow survivors along the way and getting into all kinds of trouble, as all are driven to the same central point and without knowing exactly why. That is the only common thread among these major protagonists. There are secondary characters, necessary for conflict and to help expose the backstories of the main protagonists, but in no part of this book are these secondary characters' POVs used. I don't want to give away the story but when all the major protagonists eventually connect, there rises one only.

Keep in mind that *The Stand* has over 800 pages which would allow 200 pages each for four separate protagonists — almost four separate novels for the rest of us, right?

So yes. We CAN, we *may*, get away with using multiple POVs, but while learning the craft of storytelling, it's best to do it the hard way first: stick with one protagonist until we get really good at sticking with one.

"You got my text…but did you get my *subtext*?"

Subtext — Talkin' Dirty

Oh, the scenes we could write using this cartoon!

Text/subtext: "Let's meet at McDonald's [where we had that big break-up fight because you were being such an ass]."

Text/subtext: "Let's meet at Giovanni's [where we had that amazing dinner by candlelight and after which we spent the whole night exhausting each other making mad passionate love]."

Subtext belongs in dialogue. I can think of no other place for it. Therefore, I'll cite screenwriting examples because screenplays are full of subtext (or should be). [Incidentally, I highly recommend studying several — repeat, several — books on screenwriting. Guaranteed, it will improve your story-writing skills immeasurably.]

Here are some examples. I particularly recommend Eric Edson's *The Story Solution: 23 Actions All Great Heroes Must Take*.

In novels, subtext is especially lovely in the Romance genre, particularly when the lovers first meet. I need not say how much fun subtext is in the horror genre, either in film or in books.

My first experience with subtext (I was 16) was the movie *Psycho*. *Psycho* is full of subtext, so much so, that if you know the ending, it almost becomes a comedy rather than a horror movie. (Well, to someone with my twisted sense of humour, that is.)

"My mother is not herself today."

Subtext is blatant truth disguised.

Here's a scene from the 1953 movie *From Here to Eternity*. Karen (Deborah Kerr) is the wife of Holmes and it is rumoured that she has had many lovers and it appears that her husband encourages this. Warden (Burt Lancaster) has seen her earlier; she doesn't wear a bra. Holmes is Warden's superior officer.

INT. CAPTAIN'S OFFICE - DAY

MEDIUM SHOT WARDEN AND HOLMES: It is a gloomy, rainy day and the lights are on in the office.

Warden is at his desk, working. Holmes is buckling on his trench coat. He wears a happy smile.

>   HOLMES
> I won't be back in time to take Retreat.
>   (winks at Warden)
> Or Reveille either, probably.
>
>   WARDEN
> Yes, sir.
>
>   HOLMES
>   (strides back and forth; jovially)
> All work and no play, Sergeant. All you do
> is sit around sweating over this paper and that.
> There are other things in this world beside work.

Warden carries some official papers to Holmes's desk.

>   HOLMES (CONT'D)
>   (bending over, tying shoelace)
> You ought to get out more yourself, Warden.

Warden is looking directly at the picture of Karen on Holmes's desk.

> WARDEN
> I've been considering it.

He turns aside as Holmes straightens up.

> HOLMES
> Well, I'm going.

He claps Warden on the back fraternally.

> HOLMES (CONT'D)
> I'm leaving it in your care, Sergeant.

> WARDEN
> It'll be here when you get back.

Holmes goes out. Warden turns back to Holmes' desk. He is still holding the papers in one hand. He looks at Karen's picture, picks it up with his other hand, squints at it, considering the chances very, very carefully.

We know darned well what's going to happen, don't we?

Making a Character Loveable

According to *The Story Solution: 23 Actions All Great Heroes Must Take* by Eric Edson [http://www.thestorysolution.com/], giving a character a few of the following traits will have readers bonding to her/him like cyanoacrylate (Super Glue®). I don't think I need to say why this is a good thing.

1. courage
2. unfair injury
3. skill
4. funny
5. just plain nice
6. in danger
7. loved by friends & family
8. hardworking
9. obsessed

These speak for themselves for the most part, but we need to take note of #5: *just plain nice*. This works for a character like Gizmo in the movie *Gremlins* but please, let's not make our characters nothing *but* sweetness and light. We must give them at least one flaw.

We need not — nor should we — use all nine of the above attributes. Pick and choose according to the backstory of the protagonist without actually telling the backstory. Use the one(s) that will advance the story, contribute to subplot, add love interest, excitement, mystery, motivation …

Take, for example, the main character in RJ Harlick's Meg Harris Mysteries (http://www.rjharlick.ca/).

Meg is brave, smart, nosy, helpful, determined, curious ... all qualities essential for "detecting" perpetrators and having folks cooperate and supply information ("talk"). But she has a predilection for too much booze and a problem with close relationships. She sounds almost human, doesn't she?

RJ Harlick puts Meg in danger in every one of these mysteries and Meg's flaws add an extra element of danger (#6, above): Meg is usually alone when she hunts for the murderer and she occasionally falls off the wagon, too. Uncertainty always lurks in the shadows.

If we *must* have our protagonist be as perfect as perfect can be, perhaps we can give him one enemy [not the villain]. This enemy seems to know — or actually does know — something nasty about our just plain nice protagonist. This enemy could even be the clichéd hypercritical, gossipy next door neighbour. [It's always good to avoid the stereotype like the nosy neighbour, but some genres tolerate, if not require, clichéd secondary characters.]

Perhaps rather than have our protagonist move *into* the neighbourhood (standard fare for Romance novels, as one example) have somebody else move in. Somebody who swears they know our hero. Does our hero know her?

Making a Character Killable

In the movie *Fatal Attraction*, could we have accepted Dan's dispatching of Alex *before* she boiled the bunny?

In the Dirty Harry movies, could we have enjoyed the now-famous quotes "You have to ask yourself, do I feel lucky? Well do you? ... Punk" and "Make my day" quite as much if we hadn't wanted to kill the Antagonist just as much as Harry did?

Was I the only one who cheered out loud, alone in my living room, while watching that so-satisfying Resolution in *The Girl with the Dragon Tattoo*?

For the most part, we Earthlings are deeply moral so can rarely condone the killing of anyone, even fictional characters. We are forgiving, loving, understanding. I would venture to say that most of us who are readers possess an even higher degree of compassion — mostly because we read. So how can we possibly accept, enjoy, cheer when a character is killed off?

At the heart of us, we can't.

Unless ...

Unless the Antagonist (a.k.a., the Adversary) deserves it: is killable.

But ... We must not make the Antagonist *entirely* what some call "evil". Even serial killers have a background that helped condition them and this elicits from us a certain amount of sympathy. No one-dimensional characters, please. Even cartoon characters are in two dimensions.

Dracula is the epitome of "evil" but the poor guy is looking for a long-lost love. Ah, yes. We can easily relate to that, can't we? I always feel a bit sad when Frankenstein's Creature is killed off, too.

However, Dracula is a control freak. He wants his "long-lost love" to be the next thing to a slave — and for ever and ever — while the two of them travel the world biting people's necks and turning them, essentially, into clones of themselves: soulless wanderers of the night taking up valuable cemetery space during the day.

Frankenstein's Creature is nowhere near "evil". He's the sad result of a scientist's ambitions. We pity The Creature. We don't like seeing him die at the hands of the villagers but tell ourselves "Well, it's best, isn't it? Poor thing."

We must have our Antagonist do something absolutely despicable purely for self-centred reasons *and he must have no regrets for doing it*. He may regret getting caught. Or not. He may regret having killed the little girl. But make him regret having killed her so quickly, not for killing her in the first place.

We must not have the Killable Antagonist do anything kind, as this is what we do to make a bad guy loveable (*Save The Cat! The Last Book on Screenwriting You'll Ever Need* by Blake Snyder). It's not a good idea to kill off anyone loveable — unless by a character who is killable. [Or to ratchet up sympathy for a character who loses someone they love.]

Unless ...

Unless the Killable Antagonist's motivation is purely selfish. "Oh, hello little girl. You're lost, are you? Come with me. I'll help you find Mommy ..."

Make 'em Wanna — Motivation

Bernadette wants the carrot. Bernadette reaches up and plucks one end of the bow holding the carrot. The carrot drops into Bernadette's hand.

Wonderful. A happy ending to a ... to a what exactly? An exciting story? A saleable book? Why would anybody pay good money (or even bad money) to read this story — and it is a story. It has a beginning, a middle, and an end. It contains motivation (she wants it), action (she unties the bow), a resolution (she gets the carrot).

Let's ramp it up. Let's give a reader the "motivation" to turn to the next page, shall we?

Let's say that Bernadette wants the carrot but the carrot is at the Superstore across town and it's not open yet. Ah. Now you're making your reader wonder: How will she get her carrot if the store isn't open yet? Maybe I'll turn the page to see what happens.

The reader turns the page to learn that Bernadette has no car, no bicycle and her Presto card is maxed-out so she can't even go by bus and it's too far to walk.

Dear Reader will no doubt say to himself something along the lines of: "Oh, well. I guess she doesn't get her carrot then. And do I care? Not really."

But what if ...?

1. What if it's a special magical carrot that she must keep out of the hands of the Evil Witch or Earth will be turned into a desert wasteland?
2. What if it's a special herbal carrot that will save her brother, Little Johnny, from succumbing to a rare medical condition?
3. What if the carrot is not really a carrot at all but contains a secret code to unlock the mysteries of the ancient pharaohs?

4. What if the carrot is contaminated with Ebola virus?

Even this is not enough. What if …
1. Bernadette has access to a spaceship so doesn't have to stay here when Earth is turned into a wasteland?
2. Bernadette and Little Johnny live right beside a hospital?
3. Bernadette has always hated history so doesn't care a fig about ancient pharaohs?
4. Bernadette has enough food to barricade herself in her own house until the World Health Organization guys clean up the Ebola mess?

What can we do then? How do we motivate Bernadette?
1. The spaceship needs a password …
2. In his declining mental state, Little Johnny wanders away from home …
3. Bernadette has a summer job at the museum and accidentally reads, out loud, the translation of an ancient papyrus and this wakes up the mummy on the third floor …
4. Bernadette is the only one who knows about the Ebola virus on the carrot but the cops won't believe her because her ex is a cop and told everybody she's a wacko …

We now have *four* stories worth turning pages for!

Conflict is Required

Why is conflict necessary? Without conflict, there's no story; without story, our efforts are merely lovely words strung together to form lovely sentences.

Conflict creates action and result. Action and result create change. In some cases, a character might resolve *not* to change his convictions. Is this a positive thing for a story? It depends.

Give Larry Larva in the above cartoon a reason to want to change and he may give it a try. Depends on the stakes. Depends on what has happened to create enough conflict in his life to stir things up enough to make him notice. Will he care if his wife threatens to leave him? If not, what if she will be bringing his TV with her when she goes …?

How about another scenario:

Will Judge McStoneface succumb to the threats of the Bad Guys and declare a mistrial so Chuck Rotten can get away with murder? Or will he stick to his guns and do what's right?

Perhaps Judge McStoneface has taken bribes in the past but he has fallen in love with a woman he greatly respects and has promised her never to do it again? Will he change? Or will he go back to what's familiar?

Conflict isn't only between Protagonist and Adversary. Conflict can be within a character's self as well. Stir it up. The more conflict from within and between and among characters, the better.

If a Protagonist not only has to deal with the Adversary but he's having problems at home as well, this ramps things up. Perhaps Judge McStoneface is divorced and learns:

- his son has been caught drinking and driving and the ex-wife wants the judge to pull some strings;
- is it true that his daughter is taking drugs and is getting dangerously close to prostituting herself to pay for them?
- maybe he has discovered that his ex-wife was having an affair and his son/daughter isn't his own …
- who was the affair with? with the Crown Attorney? another judge? with the only man who can help him defeat the Antagonist? with the Antagonist himself?

There are endless possibilities for creating conflict for our Protagonist.

How about this storyline? Which of these would a reader prefer?

A man and a woman meet in a grocery store:
- he is handsome and single
- she is beautiful and a widow
- they date for a few months
- they get engaged
- they marry

End of story.

A man and a woman meet in a grocery store:
- he is handsome and single
- she is beautiful and a widow
- they date for a few months
- turns out his ex-girlfriend is stalking him and wants to get the widow out of the picture
- turns out the widow's best childhood friend *is* the ex-girlfriend
- neither of the gals is aware of this just yet …
- but the man is …
- turns out the ex-girlfriend is an undercover cop (or a spy?) and wants to save the widow from the man
- turns out the man is a serial bigamist who hunts widows (or is a counterspy?)

How will we end *this* story? What if the widow isn't really a widow …? What if she's the Bad Guy? What if the man knows this but the ex-girlfriend doesn't? What if we turn this into a comedy and have everybody know everything about everybody else but for some convoluted reason nobody can divulge the information?

Yes. Conflict is required.

Dilemma = Motivation = Story!

Give your protagonist two equally unacceptable choices, then step back and let the story unfold by itself.

Pete's 1st Dilemma: In his rubber dinghy, Pete Pig floats up to an isolated island to learn that it's already inhabited. Although he hasn't had food for days, and there appears to be vegetation on the island for him to eat (the man's easily accessible kilt for one), Pete knows by the look of the man standing there, that the man could be just as hungry as he is. Pete is pork. Pete is food.

Which holds the greater risk? The sea? Or the island?

Isaac's 1st Dilemma: Isaac is sick of eating coconuts and hasn't been able to catch any fish. He is getting weaker and weaker. He needs protein and a good bit of protein has just washed up onto shore in a rubber dinghy. However, this protein is in the form of pork and because Isaac is a Jew, he does not eat pork.

And on top of that, he's a rabbi and even if there is no one else on the island to give good example to, he must follow his conscience. *Although,* he reminds himself, *there are times when laws may be broken to save a life, even one's own.*

Is this one of those times? Or not?

Pete's 2nd Dilemma: If Pete chooses to go ashore and the man attacks Pete and he has to kill the man in self-defence, who will climb the tree to get the leaves for Pete to eat? How often do coconuts fall off on their own? Who will crack open the coconuts for Pete to get at the water inside them?

If the man attacks and Pete kills him, Pete's dead. If Pete doesn't defend himself, he's dead.

Isaac's 2nd Dilemma: Isaac is aware that pigs are omnivores. He's heard stories about pigs eating human flesh. This pig looks strong enough —and hungry enough — to overwhelm Isaac.

If Isaac is forced to kill the pig in self-defence, it would be a waste of food if he didn't consume the flesh — so he might as well kill the pig immediately, just in case. But what if it's a tame pig? Not dangerous? What if he could turn it into a pet? A companion. G_d knows it's lonely here without having a guilty conscience on top of everything else.

Should Isaac allow the pig to come ashore? Or not?

Pete's 3rd Dilemma: When Pete takes a closer look at the man and sees the yarmulke and sidelocks, he relaxes somewhat. If Pete is right, and the man is a Jew, Pete most likely will not be on the menu.

We can develop a friendship in that case, decides Pete. Work together. I'm the one with the raft after all. I have fishing gear but no opposable thumbs to use it.

However ... He might not want to cook me up for food, but I'd make great bait to fish with. I'd also make a great signal for passing ships if he set me on fire … with the matches hidden in my little boat here.

Do I reveal everything all at once? Or a little at a time. Maybe keep the matches hidden for now?

Isaac's 3rd Dilemma: Once Isaac turns the pig into his pet, and teaches him some obedience lessons, maybe the pig would allow him to carve off one of its legs with the clam shell Isaac's been using as a knife. This would provide a bit of food. But Isaac knows that would be causing great pain to a living being and this is something he cannot do. *And how would I stop the bleeding anyway? I might as well kill him immediately ... But that wouldn't be right.*

Then Isaac wonders how many coconuts and leaves the pig would eat in a day. Can this island sustain the two of them? Isaac has seen a first aid kit tucked into a far corner of the pig's little raft and what looks like a fishing kit in the other. If the pig comes ashore, they can both obtain sustenance from fish and clams and seaweed.

Should Isaac take the chance? Or not?

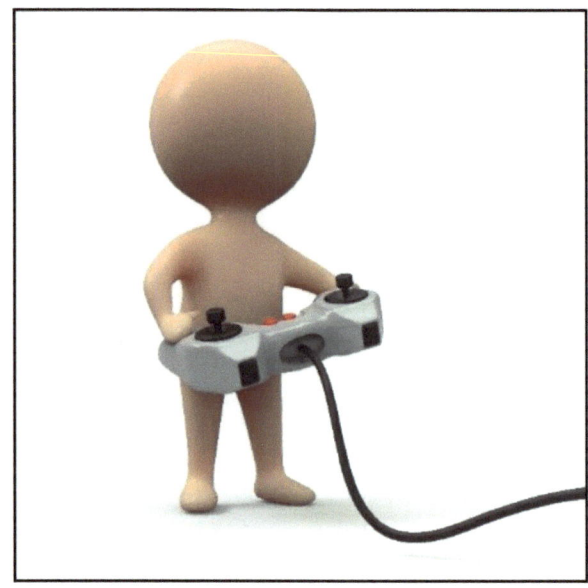

Go Ahead — Manipulate Your Readers

The Best Authors Are the Best Manipulators

It's all about what we put into people's heads without having them notice that we're doing it. We have to make them **trust** us so they'll follow us into whatever world we want to lead them.

Why would an author want to manipulate his readers?

Let me put it another way: Why would an author want his readers unable to stop themselves from turning the pages? Unable to control their fear, their pleasure, their curiosity? Unable to control the need to run out and buy this author's [*yours?*] next book and isolate themselves once again on this author's story-island?

We want it. We do. And it's all about our choice of words. Seriously. That's it. That's all.

Easy-peasy, right?

Mm. Maybe not.

In order to manipulate the reader with words, we have to know the meanings of words.

I think it was in Grade 9 that I read a dictionary from aa to the end of z. (Back in those days we had only TV — and one channel at that — to distract us.)

There are so very many lovely, delicious, enticing, amazing words, aren't there? Like *pilgarlic*, for example. This is the first time since 1959, that I've been able to actually use it. *Hooray*. How exciting. And I don't think I'll ever be able to use it again.

Why?

Let's say I wish to inject a mood or tell the reader something about Theresa in a passage, maybe both.

For the first time in person, Theresa is meeting a man she met on an online dating site:

"Yes," she told the host. "The window seat is perfect. Thank you." From this vantage point she would be able to watch for FaithfulMan271 — no matter from which direction he came — and size him up without his noticing her doing it.

But as she waited and waited, the pilgarlic staring at her from the farthest corner of the dark restaurant began to make her nervous. Had she made the right decision to meet FaithfulMan271 in this part of the city?

Now, first of all, most readers won't know the meaning of pilgarlic and will have to look it up. (Here's the definition: http://www.merriam-webster.com/dictionary/pilgarlic) Most won't bother. If they do, they will need to decide: Is the narrator intending the first use of the definition of pilgarlic? *A bald man*? Or the second: *a man looked upon with humorous contempt or mock pity*?

I would assume the second definition if this section of the book is supposed to convey that Theresa is a snooty, judgemental little bitch.

I would assume the former if FaithfulMan271 lied on the dating site [*no! really?*] and also put up a picture of his much, much younger self, and has made certain to arrive first so he can check Theresa out and make his escape if she is not up to snuff*. The first definition might also indicate that Theresa is a sweet young *thang* being stalked by a bald man. (Using "bald man" in this case, would give an author a great way to have the stalking antagonist easily spotted in a crowd.)

But forcing our reader to stop in mid-sentence to look up a word in the first place, then have to decide which definition is intended, is just plain mean. (In this case, I'm using "mean" as a euphemism for "stupid".)

I've been a voracious reader since forever. I was a typesetter for 20 years, of a great deal of government gobbledygook — in both official languages — as well as typesetting scientific journals for eight of those years. So I know (understand) a lot of words. But when I am reading a book with an enticing title that leads me to believe this book will be some kind of fast-paced adventure, and discover to my disappointment that I have to meander through a forest of florid, flamboyant, ornate, fancy, convoluted, high-flown, high-sounding, magniloquent, grandiloquent, baroque, orotund, overblown words just for the guy to put the garbage out at the curb, I will sadly set the book aside until later. Much later. Maybe even lend this book to that friend who never returns them …

We must use words that will trigger primitive responses in our readers. Single-meaning words that the eye will use as stepping stones across the sea of their imagination to the shore of our story-island are best.

---

*up to snuff has two very different meanings, one British, one North American. And no, silly, we aren't allowed to use footnotes in our novels.

Be Kind to Your Critters

Be Nice to Your Readers

Don't make loveable anybody you're planning to kill off in the first few pages. A reader won't **trust** you anymore, and a reader has to be able to trust you in order to **suspend disbelief**. And to read the rest of the story.

Along the same lines, try not to kill off the **family pet** unless you're dealing with a really **despicable antagonist**. The term "bunny boiler" has come into use on Internet dating sites to describe a woman who becomes psychotically attached to a man she's had sex with. (I'll give away everything if I tell you the name of the movie that spawned the term, so I won't.)

In one of my in-progress screenplays, I kill off the dog (he's dead by around page/minute 3), but that's to **warn my protagonist** not to mess around with what he's wanting to get involved in.

I have not, though, made the dog cute. I have made the dog intelligent — smart enough to know that what my protagonist is dealing with is dangerous.

The dog sacrifices himself to try to save his master. Killing off the dog during the Setup garners sympathy for my protagonist because if his dog is willing to die for him, he must be an OK guy.

This will develop oodles of **reader sympathy** for the protagonist. If we can kill off a guy's doggie, what are we going to do to our guy?

This helps to **signal the genre** as well. It's thoughtful to let your reader know when something unpleasant is lurking around the corner.

I have given the dog a name. Well, actually, my protagonist gave him the name and "Blackie" is probably the umpteenth dog named Blackie that Jeremiah and his wife have owned. (Back story: Jeremiah is a no-frills kinda guy who has been hiding in the bush with his beloved Margaret for years.)

If you're going to kill a person or a pet, give them a **generic name**. It makes it easier on you and on your reader.

Besides, if you go to all the trouble of coming up with something unique, it would be a waste to use it for only a page or two. Save it for somebody/something that will live until at least Chapter 10.

Yes, We Can Be Too Nice

By all means, let us expunge racism, judgement, selfishness, superiority, envy, criminal thought and any sort of meanness from our own psyches, but let us feel free to load these delicious attributes high on top of our characters. Let no character go unscathed, not even our precious protagonist. Screw political correctness for each of our characters; instead, turn them into real human beings with real thoughts and feelings.

If there are no conflicts or difficulties or if nothing happens to anybody, what's the point of reading a story? What's the point of writing it?

The Nice Three Little Pigs

Once upon a time there were Three Little Pigs who worked together to build three houses out of donated materials for homeless pigs. The building inspector came along and even though some of the work was shoddy and the equipment far from standard, he didn't want to hurt the feelings of these hard workers so he put <u>Passed Inspection</u> stickers on each of the three houses. Everyone lived happily ever after.

The Nice Little Red Riding Hood

Once upon a time there was a little girl named Little Red Riding Hood. That wasn't her real name, but because her loving grandmother had made her a red cape, everyone called her that. One day she was walking to her grandmother's house with a basket of vegetables and one of Granny's neighbours saw her and ran ahead to tell Granny to get out of her night clothes and get dressed for company. A woodsman saw the neighbour do this, so he gathered up the wood he had chopped and ran to the house with it so there would be a lovely fire in the fireplace for company. Everyone lived happily ever after.

The Nice Goldilocks & the Three Bears

Once upon a time there was a little girl named Goldilocks. She went for a walk in the woods one day and came to a cabin. She thought of going inside to look around but knew that it would be considered Breaking & Entering if she did, so she sat on the porch and waited. Before long, a lovely couple with their son arrived and invited her in. They enjoyed tea and chocolate cake and then she went back home. Everyone lived happily ever after.

If these stories had been written like this, would they have affected us as children so deeply? Hardly!

I recently recalled a story my mother would remind me of at chore time, "Remember what happened to those lazy ones in 'The Little Red Hen', Sherrill. She did all the work so the lazy ones got nothing." Being reminded of this story certainly made me feel guilty enough to pitch in and try to do even more of my share for fear of abandonment and starvation. (For those of you who are not familiar with it, here's a link: http://www.enchantedlearning.com/stories/fairytale/littleredhen/story/)

I cannot tell you how strong a work ethic this story inspired in me (no doubt because of how scarily it was presented). Imagine if this story had been written with sweetness and light, written with niceness. Would I have identified with the dog, the cat or the duck back when I was seven or eight years old? Of course, I would have. I preferred to go out and play with my friends, not set the table and do the dishes and tidy up after my little sister.

Once upon a time there was a Little Red Hen who found some grain in her yard. She planted it and harvested it, took it to the mill for grinding, made bread out of it and handed it out to her friends and neighbours for free. Everyone lived happily ever after.

[Please note that including this last story — or any of the others — is not meant as any kind of political statement. And including this note in the first place is not meant as any kind of political statement either. I'm citing Mom's warnings to show how a story that includes characters with faults can affect a story, therefore a reader/readee. Another note is that I think I heard recently that fairy tales and fables are now considered to be "inappropriate for children". Did I imagine that?]

If we want to touch our readers as deeply as possible, we must toss out "niceness" and bring into our characters figurative halitosis and smelly armpits at the very least.

An Opinion for EVERY Character

EVERY character has an attitude. An author MUST show this through **Action** and **Dialogue**. Or **Action Alone**, never dialogue alone. Why? Mere chatter is not an attitude. We need to throw some body language into it.

Every character has an opinion about what's going on. Even the bystanders. Let the reader **see** it. Perhaps one of these …?

1. A **smarmy look** from an Extra (or equivalent) in a crowd.
2. The stereotype is the gum-snapping, **confrontational waitress** with a hand on one hip (let's not do this, but look what it did for *Five Easy Pieces*).
3. A **slouch** as in the cartoon above.
4. **Bratiness**. A parent could be reprimanding a teenage son at the breakfast table and the younger son makes faces behind Mom's back trying to get his older sibling to laugh.
5. Cops head into a bad section of the city. The guy behind the desk of the rundown hotel (hooker palace) **tosses the key** to the suspect's room onto the counter instead of handing it over politely.
6. The self-righteous nosy old biddy with her **nose in the air** when she encounters teenagers doing pretty much anything that teenagers do.

Dialogue is not necessary — **show** don't tell — but here are some tips from Eric Edson's *The Story Solution: 23 Actions All Great Heroes Must Take*:

1. Dialogue should **advance dramatic conflict** that takes place in the here and now.
2. Dialogue should **hum** with dramatic tension.

3. Generally dialogue should verbalize only **one thought** at a time.
4. Good dialogue frequently conveys **subtext**.
5. Describe the **physical action**.
6. Dialogue should come out of the lives, joys, and pain of **unique characters**.
7. **Avoid small talk.**
8. Dialogue should be **brief**.
9. Character must be **demonstrated**, not described.
10. **Avoid history lessons**.
11. **Don't preach**.

(http://www.amazon.com/The-Story-Solution-Actions-Heroes/dp/1615930841)

The more attitude a character has, the more conflict is introduced into the story and therefore the more interest along with it.

An attitude need not always be a cranky one. Examples of other attitudes we can insert into any of our characters are: dignity, fear, joy, love, need, curiosity. Consider the **Seven Deadly Sins** as a source: Lust, Gluttony, Greed, Sloth, Wrath, Envy, Pride; and the **Seven Virtues**: Chastity, Temperance, Charity, Diligence, Patience, Kindness, Humility.

Pandora's Safety Deposit Box.

Don't Muzzle Your Characters

Excerpt from *How to Write a Book: Park it, Get to Work*

Many of us are sweet people who write the most gentle of stories, poems, and prose. We speak softly and would never dream of offending anyone. It isn't in us to do so. We are genuine. We are thoughtful. We wouldn't dream of being politically incorrect even in our own nightmares.

We are not uninformed. We watch the news on TV. We hear stories of murder and mayhem and earthquakes and death and dismemberment and dog attacks and sex crimes and domestic violence, even what goes on in prisons. We read books, sometimes naughty books. Some of us have children, so obviously we know there's such a thing as sex. We might even consider ourselves to be unshockable.

Can we write from the bad-guy perspective? From inside his evil head? Thinking and putting vile thoughts onto paper? Of course we can. But will we? Often we're afraid to. This is why I prefer not to write in 1st Person. It stymies. I don't want to have to be afraid or guilty when I'm writing. I want my writing to be free-flowing and most of all, a hundred percent "true".

How can we un-muzzle our characters? How can we go into our own depths to retrieve dark, negative, violent thoughts, ideas, and emotions that might be lurking in there? All those things we were told were bad when we were kids? Because of our experiences, our programming, and even our instincts (amygdalae), we are afraid of our own minds, terrified of what's in there — or what *might* be in there. Writers are further cursed with fertile imaginations.

One of the several valuable things I finally understood by Doing My Writing [See chapter De-Stressing] was that we store experiences by their emotional impact. Think of our guard-dog amygdalae [See chapter on De-Stressing.]. Since it's probably easiest to picture our head being full of filing cabinets, or drawers, please bear with me when I refer to things that way.

Our brain tends to be organized, it prefers to file like with like. Losses go into the same drawer whether it's the loss of a friend, a parent, a beloved pet, a plant, or a set of keys. One of the most basic fears hmans have is the fear of abandonment — of being without, of being alone, on our own. Anything that triggers that fear, goes into the same drawer.

The experience goes into the drawer as an emotion, the same emotion *experienced at the time of filing*. This is very important. If you loved, it goes into the Love Drawer; if you were angry, it goes into the Anger Drawer, if you were afraid, it goes into the Fear Drawer. Perhaps I can explain best with an example: I had reached an impasse Doing My Writing and had been unable to allow myself to write about the barn on my grandfather's farm. I would have been very young when something happened to me, perhaps two or younger? I could not force myself to go there. I was terrified to dredge that memory out of my subconscious mind.

My fear was so overwhelming that my adult mind told me I must have been sexually assaulted in there, or I must have seen something horrendous take place in that barn — a murder, a rape. There was no dissuading me from that idea. Something terrible had happened to me in that barn.

But I trusted my Guide (Guardian Angel, Great Spirit, Higher Power, God, Allah, Inner Self, whatever you want to call it), and forged onward. Eventually, I got through the huge barn doors: so high they were, so heavy. The barn smelled of cow poop and it was warm with cow urine. Comforting they were, giving milk, their oxytocin wafting into the atmosphere. It felt good.

I watched as Grandpa and Uncle John dexterously removed milking machines from this cow's teats to put them onto another's teats. They were so good at it, it was almost like a dance. The cows were happy as they chewed at the small piles of grain and hay in the wooden boxes in front of them. I could hear them chew. I could hear their breathing.

"WHAT ARE YOU DOING? GET AWAY FROM THERE!" Grandpa yelled at me.

He'd never raised his voice to me. I was devastated. Uncle John rushed to grab me sobbing with terror now, out of the kicking space of the Clydesdale I was standing behind, small, invisible.

When we file it, we file it with a child's emotion. When we bring it out, we see it with an adult's eyes.

But whenever we open that drawer to put a new experience in it, everything that was in there flies out — Pandora's box — and must be put back in. What a good time to reorganize our experiences in light of today. That's why loss, for instance, can seem so debilitating sometimes. We aren't experiencing only the current loss, we are re-experiencing *all* our losses simultaneously. Take them all out. Examine them. Keep the ones you want. Throw the rest away.

Ninety-nine percent of us need have no fear of going deep inside ourselves to see what's in there that might be useful for building a character. You might be very happy discovering that it wasn't really an invading space alien that lurked in your room every night when you tried to sleep, it was a mosquito — but your mother was terrified of malaria because of *her* unresolved experiences. Ninety-nine percent is not a hundred percent. I know there are indeed those who have suffered terrible things, and that the pain of reliving some of those experiences would be almost unbearable alone, without professional help. But I will say that taking something out of you that was put in there when you were a child, and looking at it now, as an adult, can be unbelievably liberating.

Here's something to practise with:

SCENARIO

Character 1: A store clerk, Mary, is an old school chum of Brenda. She recognizes Brenda right away. Why?
Character 2: Brenda is a kleptomaniac. Brenda does not recognize Mary, the store clerk. Why not?

Exercise 1
Pretend you are inside Mary's head looking out at Brenda. Did she like Brenda in school? Did she look down on her? Did Brenda admire her? Was Mary one of the popular girls perhaps, and Brenda a dowdy nerd without friends? Be inside Mary's head as she wonders what Brenda is doing now for a living, if Brenda is married, if she can believe her eyes that Brenda is actually stuffing that blouse into her large purse! Be inside Mary's head as she wonders what to do.

Exercise 2
Pretend you are Brenda stealing things. Will Brenda be upset, perhaps thinking of how mean her mother, or father, or sister, or brother, or husband, or child was to her that morning? She stuffs the blue silk blouse with the beautiful pattern on it into her purse, then suddenly recognizes Mary from … where? Somewhere. Was it pleasant? Unpleasant? Have Brenda notice Mary watching her stuff the blouse into her purse. Be inside Brenda's head as she reacts to being seen attempting to steal the blouse. Does she care?

Try both exercises in different ways: (1) Mary's mean; (2) Brenda's mean; (3) they're both mean.

"Before we start, shall we go round the table, and each share our name and a horrible dark secret from our past."

Using Backstory without Using It

The importance of **backstory** cannot be overemphasized. It's a real joy when we create **a character that comes alive** and starts going her own way, thinking on her own, and making decisions. When it happens, we can pat ourselves on the back.

What is backstory? It's everything we (author) know about our character that never makes it into the final product. Because? It has nothing to do with the current story.

Why bother with it then?

The more backstory we **know** about each character the better. With all this information for each of our characters, we'll have an easier time with:

- dialogue
- description
- action(s)
- motivation
- bonding (for both writer and reader)
- bonding (with other characters)

- inter-character relationships
- predictability
- storyline
- background
- subtext

A Trick to Help Develop Backstory: Ask Questions

This can be a lot of fun. Make up twenty or thirty questions, or more, to ask a character. For a crime story, let's interrogate them; use a rolled-up newspaper if they're the least bit uncooperative. For spy novel characters, we can follow them around to see what they do when nobody's looking — or why not inject them with Sodium Pentothal? If romance is the genre, take her out to lunch and get her drinking white wine and talking about her ex or her previous job or what she wants in a partner.

Most of this will never make it into the actual story, of course — and shouldn't — but we must know our characters this well. Even the minor ones.

Knowing all this about a character will help especially with dialogue and action because we will know them so very, very well, that everything they say or do will just slip off the ends of our fingers as we write. Anything that doesn't match with who they really are will feel false so we won't even write it. (**It will save major editing time later.**)

Here's are some suggestions for a list of questions to ask our characters:

1. What's your second name? Why did your parents give you that name?
2. Did you ever make fun of anybody in your neighbourhood/school when you were a kid? Did anybody ever make fun of you when you were a kid?
3. How many men/women have you slept with? Why so many? Why so few?
4. Is there anything that could ever prompt you to take someone's life?
5. Do you like cats? What kind of cat do you like? What kind of cat do you most hate?
6. Have you ever owned a dog? How did it die?
7. Do you have any allergies?
8. Have you ever cheated on an exam?
9. Have you ever cheated on a spouse/boyfriend/girlfriend?
10. Did you ever wish you were the opposite sex?
11. Were you popular in school?
12. Were you unpopular in school?
13. What's your IQ? Do you give a shit about IQs?
14. How do you feel about swearing? What's your favourite swear word?
15. What's your favourite colour?
16. What's your favourite article of clothing?
17. Would you ever join a nudist colony?
18. Did you have a happy childhood? Why? Why not?

19. How much money do you make? What is the source of your money?
20. Are you happy?
21. Do you trust the police?
22. Do you believe in God? If you do, what do you call this Being?
23. Do you do drugs? How much?
24. Do you drink alcoholic beverages? What kind? How often? How many?
25. Have you ever tried an Internet dating site? (How did you make out?)
26. What angers you the most?
27. What turns you on the most?
28. What excites you the most?
29. What's your greatest fear?
30. Can you sing?
31. Have you ever gone fishing?
32. Can you cook?
33. Do you have a favourite fast food?
34. Do you believe in reincarnation?
35. Do you believe in soul mates?
36. Do you believe in half-souls?
37. Would you kill a bug? A ladybug? A mosquito? A spider? A butterfly?
38. Who was your first love?
39. Have you ever been kissed?
40. Who gave you your first kiss?
41. If you could be an animal, which one would it be?
42. If you could be a plant, which one would it be?
43. Where were you born?
44. Were you wanted?
45. Did you enjoy school?
46. Did/do you like your parents?
47. Did/do you like your siblings?
48. Did/do you like your spouse?
49. What's a geranium?

(Adapted from *How to Write a Book: Park it, Get to Work*)

"See?! I TOLD you!"

Describe without Details

Place

We may describe a scene or a background to develop an **atmosphere**, a <u>feel</u> for the scene we are writing, but we must maintain restraint. Pages and pages on the colour of trees and long winding roads, etc., are no longer de rigueur in novels — except in literature class. Let us eschew the hell out of doing this, even for gothic novels.

Marcel St-Amand, author of the Lemon Ultra action-adventure series, is a master at providing **just enough detail** to set a scene's required mood. From Book 2, Lemon Ultra: The Road to the Salt Mine:

> *When they finally emerged from the gorge, the landscape of the Kalash Valley presented itself like a majestic forgotten world and it was breathtaking. The Hindu Kush Mountains towered above the valley below with their snowcapped walls, and Himalayan cedar forests painted the rest of the mountains. Houses, sanctuaries, and fields gripping the hillsides combined with meandering streams that sparkled like some sort of precious necklace of pearls. It was a picture of a lost nation.*

With one short paragraph (four sentences) about this place, the author has triggered the storage facility in our right brain (the concept side) and we can feel it, understand its loneliness, its sorrow, its isolation, its power, its danger.

Character

We need not describe a character in great detail, either. In fact, it's usually **not a good idea** at all.

Again, from Marcel St-Amand's Lemon Ultra: The Road to the Salt Mine:

> *He heard a scrape of footwear coming close to him, then his hood came off. A man stood in front of him, dressed in Mujahideen fashion complete with a pakul that sat slightly back on his head. He was a young man with eyes as dark as charcoal and which had an intensity of conviction. The young man's thin hands—almost out of place as they really belonged to an office joe—held an Avtomat Kalashnikova, an AK-47 Soviet rifle, with a firm grip. The weapon, with its distinctive magazine that curved outward, had seen better years as grunge had built up on the stock and the barrel was in need of bluing but still, it rendered that sad patina gained from daily usage. When Peter's eyes adjusted, he realized he was indeed in a small grotto.*

Note that Mr St-Amand has described only:
- the young man's clothing
- the colour of his eyes
- his hands
- the weapon he holds

… but we can see all of him in our mind; it feels like we know a lot about him; we are afraid.

Note

It is best to eliminate ALL physical descriptions <u>that pertain to Race</u> — unless it's important to the story. Readers like to imagine they are the character as they read. If our characters — especially our main characters — are described as White/Black/Asian, we are alienating potential readers.

Relatively recent world stats on population by Race are:
- Asian 54%
  - East Asian 24% (Korea, Mongolia, China, Japan)
  - South Asian 21% (India, Sri Lanka, Pakistan, Bangladesh, Nepal)
  - Southeast Asian 9% (Cambodia, Burma, Philippines, Malaysia)
- Black 15%
- White 15%
- Hispanic 8%
- Middle Eastern 8%

Before the First Edit, Make a List of Characters

Beside each name, let's write the way we have first described physically each of our characters: main, secondary, tertiary and beyond.

How many have long flowing golden locks and flashing blue eyes?

Oops.

Instead, describe the character's character — no doubt where the term "character" came from in the first place. How about something like:

The deep-fryer that was born of some inner rage sizzled off him.

Continue to think of this guy in terms of, e.g.:
- hot temper
- hot bod
- is he a chef?

… but don't continue with the simile. It will become tiresome.

In General

Watch out for a procession of adjectives

the large, expansive, far-reaching meadow stretched before him.

... because these adjectives are usually redundant and lead the writer through the malapropism mine field.

What's wrong with ...?

the meadow stretched before him.

Mantra: I will not be lazy. I will use the right noun/verb. I will not fluff up my sentences with extra words explaining things. I WILL BE CONFIDENT! I will not be lazy. I will use the right noun/verb. I will not fluff up my sentences with extra words …

Describe through Action

Actions Show Character and/or Motivation

From How to Write a Book: Park it, Get to Work

*Because we know everything about our character, we know why he does what he does. The reader won't care a whit that Bill was frightened by a dog when he was three years old because that would get in the way of the story. But we (as the writer) know that when Roger chases Bill out of the restaurant and Bill jumps that fence, and there's a dog in that yard, Bill will lose ground by running as far around the dog as he can instead of on a straight line past it. When Roger follows him, Roger will run right past the dog — perhaps even jump over it — to catch up with Bill and tackle him. The reader doesn't need to know **why** Bill is afraid of dogs, only **that** Bill is afraid of dogs.*

Readers Are Intelligent. They Don't Need Things Spelled Out

She <u>stepped into the slaughterhouse and</u> immediately wrinkled her nose. It smelled like dead animals in there.

Do we need the underlined bit in the above passage? Slaughterhouse = dead animals. Wrinkled her nose = something reeks.

Actions Show Physical Characteristics

Let's go to a library for a minute.

If we know exactly what Janey, our librarian, looks like, we won't be making the mistake of having her extend her arm horizontally to the second shelf from the top of the stack to grab a book if she's only 4′10″. We don't have to tell anybody how tall she is, they will **see** how tall she is **by her actions**.

Janey rose to her tiptoes to place a kiss on Tony's lips.

Janey bent down to place a kiss on the top of Mikey's head.

How tall is Janey, relatively speaking? How tall is Tony? How tall is Mikey?

For a Reader, Familiarity Breeds Content

It's important to give as much information about a character as we can as this makes them familiar (like family) to the reader, but rhyming off a series of characteristics will leave a reader cold. If they want a list of traits, they'll read non-fiction.

Compare using details:

Tom was an old man. He was over six feet tall. He used to be an auto mechanic in his home town, Shaw Falls. He was very friendly so everybody in town knew him and liked him. He was a really nice man.

… with using actions

Whenever Tom sauntered along Shaw Falls' main street on his daily morning walk, he would pause to chat with almost everyone he met along the way, both parties smiling warmly. Tom would take these opportunities to lean on his cane, his gnarled hands still bearing years-old grease in their knuckles' cracks. Shaking with the effort of pulling breath into exhaust-fume-damaged lungs, he would curl his bent shoulders down, especially for the children, to get his ear closer to their words so he could reply to their questions with accuracy.

I suddenly like this old guy. I think he needs a love interest …

Restraint

We mustn't throw in any old thing to get this business of describing with action working. Create the opportunity to **show** character, toss in a **bread crumb**, or **advance the plot**.

And always "beware of unmotivated actions." — James Scott Bell.

Blame it on Writer's Block

Sculptor's block

Back in the old days when writers wrote things out in longhand then either typed these pages up themselves or paid out good money to have someone else do it for them, it must have felt like they couldn't change a single word without causing a great deal of anguish.

Enter the computer. No more need for Wite-Out® or scissors and Scotch® tape. We could cut and paste and re-type to our hearts' content. Hooray! Life is good!

So why do we still have so-called Writer's Block? What is so frightening about writing when we can always change everything so easily?

I can think of two scenarios: (1) we're afraid of What Others Might Think, or (2) we're afraid of What Others Might Think.

I will qualify that last statement by adding "consciously" to one scenario and "subconsciously" to the other. Does that feel about right?

I'm working on a six-book historical novel series. The history is there; all I need to do is throw my already-created characters into it to see what happens. So what stops me sometimes? Besides Real Life (busy with choir or shopping or socializing), I mean?

My Muse throws ideas at me constantly. I awaken in the middle of the night with story ideas and I e-mail or text these to myself. I awaken some mornings with a mind full of story ideas and rush to my supply of Post-It®s, scribble on them and stick them all over my desk. I come up with delicious murders and killings while on certain bus routes at rush hour/non-rush hour. Talking with colleagues gives me brilliant ideas most of the time. (I hope this latter source is mutual.)

So why don't I use them all? Why do I wander from coffee maker to computer desk to window to coffee

maker to computer desk to window …?
- Yabut. I see that used all the time.
- Yabut. It's not in her character to do that.
- Yabut. That would sound like I just threw it in there. It has nothing to do with the story. I can't tie it in.
- Yabut. This ain't Sci-Fi, the genre is Historical Fiction. I can't use a light sabre. And no, I can't have a ghost show up with information, either. The genre is Historical Fiction, not Supernatural.
- Yabut. They don't even know each other, right? And in order to get them to meet, I'd have to change 99% of what I've already decided has to happen. Next book, maybe. Yes. I'll introduce them in the next book.
- Yabut. Now I have three or more fantastic story ideas that will all fit together but I have to back up and figure out how to lay out the pattern for these wonderful story threads (bread crumbs). (Happened to me in Book 2 of the Kesk8a series. Have you ever been so happy all you could do is dance for three weeks?)

This is not Writer's Block. This is writing. Yes it is

I don't think I'm the only writer who constantly has something on the back burner in his/her head. I have ideas tucked away in the oven and the stove drawer, too. On top of the microwave … Much to my dismay, sometimes, as I'd like to get them all out and onto paper so I can have room for more.

Is this Writer's Block, too? No. This is being polygamous without a commitment. Tsk. Tsk. Naughty, naughty.

We need to choose one story/book/article and be faithful to it until the end. When we get to the inevitable end of it where we almost always find it difficult to bid it adieu, it is quite acceptable [*read*, recommended] to start an affair with another story/book/article as this will entice us to hurry and finish the original so we can play with the new one. This is human nature no matter how hard we try to suppress it.

<u>Exception.</u> There are always exceptions to everything. Don't you love it? When we are trying to figure out the pattern of where the bread crumbs must go in a piece, we may dance with other stories/books/articles but like my mother always said: "Be sure to go home with the same person who brought you."

This is why it's so much fun being a writer. We can do the most unimaginable forbidden delicious things in our heads without getting into any trouble at all in Real Life — and absolutely without guilt.

Summation of Writer's Block Advice
- plug your ears to the voices of friends, family, and your self-deprecating self
- hunch over the keyboard so no one can see what you are writing
- love the one you're with until it's time to say goodbye

Two Books in One?

We have accomplished 126,000 words? Bravo! Now we need to either cut that back by editing a lot out or cut it into two different ideas, expand those to "fit" and away we go. Two books!

But as always, it depends.

For science fiction/fantasy, an author needs extra space to develop a world the reader is unfamiliar with so can be forgiven for writing lengthy tomes. Because these genres tend to run long, fans expect it. (But all the "rules" about windbaggery still apply, right? <u>Nothing goes in unless it shows character or moves the plot along.</u>)

Some Book Lengths per Genre

(Information gleaned from *Word Count for Novels and Children's Books: The Definitive Post* by Chuck Sambuchino, October 24, 2012: <u>http://www.writersdigest.com/editor-blogs/guide-to-literary-agents/word-count-for-novels-and-childrens-books-the-definitive-post</u>)

<u>Quote from the October 2012 posting:</u>

> *"But what about J.K. Rowling???" asks that man in the back of the room, putting his palms up the air. Well—remember the first Harry Potter book? It wasn't that long. After JK made the publishing house oodles and oodles of money, she could do whatever she wanted. And since most writers*

haven't earned oodles, they need to stick to the rules and make sure they [sic] *work gets read. The other thing that will make you an exception is if your writing is absolutely brilliant. But let's face it. Most of our work does not classify as "absolutely brilliant" or we'd all have 16 novels at this point.*

According to Chuck Sambuchino, who has an in with agents, these are the general word counts accepted by most Traditional Houses.
- **Adult** novels, generally, 80,000–89,999
- **SciFi and Fantasy**, 100,000–115,000
- **Middle Grade**, **'Tweens** (12-year-olds), 20,000–55,000
- **Upper Middle Grade**, 40,000–55,000
- **Young Adult** (YA), 55,000–69,999

According to the film industry:
- **Screenplays**, keep these under 120 pages (1 page = 1 minute). The best length for a screenplay is 90 pages because it allows for all the commercials to fit in there when it becomes famous and they show it on TV. ["Everything is economics."]

But, but …

What if we are Indie Authors?

Do we still need to follow these guidelines? There's no "it depends" here. **Yes.**
So what do we do when we've ended up with too many words?

Breathe! It's A Windfall

If we have done as much editing as possible and we still have well over the suggested count, why not turn our work into a series?

Series are all the rage these days. We can massage the MS into [usually] three parts and market it that way.
Because generally, e-fans prefer their reading brief, publish these parts as e-books only, not in print.

Transplant Your Head into a Commuter's for a Moment

Imagine sitting on a bus for an hour or more — each way — every weekday and looking at the same old scenery. In the winter, the windows frost up …

Then let's imagine reading one of this **new author's e-books** while travelling. Perhaps we read the first half on the way into work on a Tuesday morning. We are intrigued by the well-thought-out plot and fascinating characters so are looking forward to reading the other half on the way home. The reading time fits perfectly.

We can't *wait* to get into the second of this new author's series on Wednesday morning.

We might even start reading it at the bus stop …

"The plot is a little thin for a novel. But there may be a great *tweet* in it."

Not Enough Novel for a Novel?

Writing too many words as discussed in the last chapter can have its benefits. But what if we need a specific length and don't have enough words to fill that requirement?

1. Develop a story or two to weave in.
2. Make them form a "rope" or a "braid" toward the end.
3. Trim off the "ends" (literally!) until only the Protagonist is left then have him/her ride off into the sunset.

ta-da The End

How Am I Going to Do That?

Remember all those **story ideas** we've been writing down on index cards and storing in alphabetical order in a lovely holder we picked up at that antique shop and that we keep on the right hand side of the second shelf of the bookcase in the study? No?

OK, then …

Remember that **notebook** we've had since high school or college with scribbling in it and into which we stuff all manner of notes and story ideas written on restaurant napkins, facial tissues, scraps of paper, and right at the moment can't remember where the hell we left it?

Yes. That's the one.

Find it. Dig it out.

Sort through the story ideas and <u>any that are fairly well-developed</u> (meaning there's at least one sentence written) that are set in the …

1. same genre;
2. same venue (town, city or country);
3. same time frame; and
4. same target readership

…. <u>will be absolute</u> **GOLD!**

And they will also be absolute FUN to play with.

What Next?

Keeping the plot of our main story in mind, figure out some kind of [undisclosed as yet] backstory that will connect our new characters to the Protagonist and write their story from there.

(Each of these subplots will have its own sub-Protagonist and sub-Antagonist.)

Since we now have a goal to aim for — i.e., connecting the subplot with the main plot toward the end of the story — our writer's block should disappear for that original story. (The idea of writing a story backwards is an excellent one that I picked up from a screenwriting how-to. Unfortunately, the name of it and its author have drifted off into the ether.)

<u>An intimate **connection of subplot with main story** is crucial. The novel won't work without it.</u>

Motivations for subplot characters are paramount and usually hidden until the threads connect at the end. This is where the "fun" part comes in. I actually cackle with glee when my Muse tosses a subplot motive into my head. (She is just pure evil and that's why I love my Muse so much. xox)

How Many Subplots?

Don't go overboard with **too many subplots** because the reader's sympathy for the main Protagonist will be diminished exponentially. (This is related to my fave bugbear: POV bouncing.)

If using two subplots, it's a good idea to weave these in with each other fairly early on. Why? If we suddenly bring in all kinds of subplots all at once, our novel will look like we didn't have enough words to fill it out and just went through some old notes and tossed them in.

Too Many Cooks

Too Many *Cooks* in Our Stories

The first book I wrote had dozens and dozens of characters. Several **Protagonists**, for one thing. I had one main **Antagonist** in the "person" of The Watcher — the character who precedes the Elder God — but he had brought along with him many, many Soul Eaters from Outer Darkness who were his **Sidekicks** (for want of a better term) and my Protagonists had their own troubles with their own Antagonists and Sidekicks and there was a **huge backstory** with each and ever character on top of everything else. But wait, maybe the Elder God was the main Antagonist … Or was it the doctor? Maybe the Chief of Police was the Antagonist and the Protagonist really *was* Rachel Graye after all.

Get my drift?

I was still in the workforce at the time I was writing this opus and going through some work and personal stuff so when I got home from work each day, I would kill off yet another character. So I needed lots of them to do this. I most certainly didn't need to give *them* as much of a life (backstory) as my [several] main characters had, but I did!

What did I know? It was my first attempt at writing anything longer than a grocery list.* Well, to be perfectly honest, anything longer than fourteen-page hand-written love letters to a guy who had said he was separated but as it turned out … Yes, he died in the book, too. Horribly.

---

*More than grocery lists. Couldn't resist a stab at humour here. I actually wrote a lot of poetry, a few short stories, newspaper articles and dozens of first pages of potential books. And more poetry.

I didn't even have a typewriter until I started writing it. PCs were just slipping over the horizon into our lives and I resented the hell out of PCs. They were what would eventually cause the extinction of my trade.

I hadn't done enough research on what and what not to use for the genre. Too many cooks, too many characters, too many story threads, too many pages. **Not enough experience.** I learned an amazing amount about writing when I began studying screenplay writing. (Here they are again.)

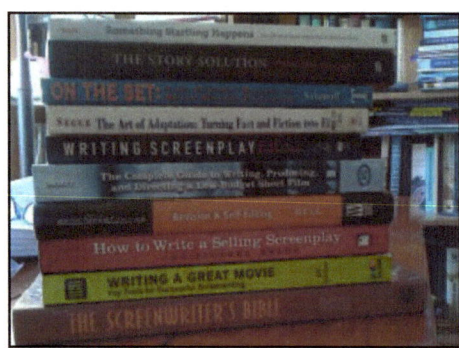

Working as an editor for almost eight years (2007–15) was also an eye-opener as far as learning what habits we writers have — every one of us! — that we need to eschew. (My typesetting background provided the necessary qualifications for editing and designing Indie Authors' books.) I don't edit anymore — it's much too time consuming. I have a pile of my own work to do almost as high as the pile in the photo — but I still design. For me, that's playtime.

Despite the mess of my first novel, I was greatly rewarded for working all the way through it. I've been able to get several screenplays (one completed; two in the works, one still in my head) and a couple of short stories out of all these extras. *Plus* a great little town to set many of my books, screenplays and stories in: Shaw Falls. Oodles of characters that I know intimately and who will come in handy as primary, secondary, or even tertiary *people* in future works.

Never fret about using too many characters in the **first draft**. Remove them in the **first edit** and set them aside for their own stories or novels or screenplays in the future. In fact, never fret about anything in the first draft. Just plug on until you get to the end. Then go back and **fix** it all. Then fix it again. Use your strays to multiply your books and stories.

Recycling Characters

Story Idea but Don't Know Where to Begin?

Instead of sitting there looking at a blank screen as you try to begin your next work, grab one of those **minor** characters from your last novel — how about the gas jockey, the one your main character asked for directions? Have him come into a vast inheritance, clean him up a bit, give him a shave, a new hairstyle, make him avoid an accident while driving his Porsche along some back road, end up in the ditch, have a charming young country bumpkin pull up in the tow truck …

You won't have to do any research on him at all. You've already done it. Perhaps you might use a minor female character from one of your other novels — one set in the city. Hmm. Maybe that "country bumpkin" isn't so country after all.

Easy-peasy when we have so much of the hard slogging already done, isn't it?

But!

Do as I Say, Not as I Did

We mustn't include a lot of backstory in the actual story itself. Best to imply it; have a neighbour mention something; have a snarky comment come up in a patch of conflict-ridden dialogue, a comment that indicates there's … yes, more to the story! **Show. Don't tell.**

As previously mentioned, I spent years writing my first novel and I gave a backstory to every single character in it. And some of these characters existed only to be killed by The Watcher or the Soul Eaters that followed him around. They were Extras. That's all.

I had one bad guy, The Watcher, and a bunch of minor bad guys, the Soul Eaters. Both The Watcher and the Soul Eaters were henchmen (henchpersons?) of the *really* bad guy, one of the Elder Gods (not *one* Elder God, no, there were several to choose from).

I gave each of my characters a full life in the actual novel, and managed to entwine everything into the story. Uh. More or less.

Even a guy named Dave, who was an only *mentioned* woman's husband, had his back story included. The novel was way too complicated for the storyline so bogged it down. Bogged it down? Dragged it bloody backwards!

The Good News?

Most of us wonder how Stephen King can be so prolific in his writings. I'm a fan, so have read pretty much all of his works and know that he sets most of them in the same area (Maine), often refers to characters from other books, like store owners or sheriffs, etc., so he no doubt hangs on to most of his minor characters, too. SK fans like his books because he makes us feel like we are in **familiar territory** with **familiar people** who are real to us.

So by all means, create **extensive backstories** for everyone and keep them on file. You can pull them out in the future as full-blown characters in their own books, movies, and stories.

Dave (the dismemberee from my vast opus mentioned above) made it into *The Soul Eaters* screenplay as a fully developed supporting character. Your work won't go to waste unless you let it.

Making Your Grammar App Weep

One of the things I ran across occasionally when editing fiction MSs (manuscripts) was narrative that reads like the author has obeyed every suggestion that his/her grammar application has pointed out. This makes for extremely boring narrative.

Some computer writing programs point out only basic grammatical errors. Others are more eager to nitpick. (It is possible to change the settings of most grammar apps (applications). See Appendix 2.)

No matter how sophisticated the app, however, a machine can't grasp the actual *meaning* of the sentence so this is why their "recommendations" are occasionally off base. Need I suggest using caution? Also, and this might surprise you: these programs don't have much of a grasp of some of the underlying obscure grammar rules, either, like the difference between gerunds ("ing" words that [usually] take the possessive case) and participles ("ing" words that do not). Just last week, my app was arguing with me about it's and its — and this is my favourite error to seek as an editor so I know I was right. But I did have a brief nightmare about WHY the app was so insistent.

I am not criticizing these apps in any way. The programmers will be able to perfect what we writers (fiction, especially) need when science perfects a thinking robot with emotions.

One thing the program I use is eager to point out (Microsoft Word because I happen to like it for editing) is what it considers to be run-on sentences. When it can't find spellos or common grammatical errors, I suppose it feels duty bound to bug me about something else.

But I have to smile when I think of Patricia K. McCarthy's grammar app's mental health. In Ms McCarthy's very popular Crimson Crimes series (http://www.patriciakmccarthy.com/), Granny, a recurring character, talks in nothing *but* run-on sentences and with no regard for even the proper words sometimes. Malapropisms abound when Granny waxes forth. Poor, dear grammar app: "Did you mean [such and such]?" "Run-on sentence!" "Consider revising!" "Did you mean [such and such]?" "Run-on sentence!" "Consider revising!"

Writing programs also have a terrible time with fractured sentences.

One of my clients writes with a unique and beautiful flowing cadence:

> *There was something about the way he strolled through the halls with his hands in his pockets, the way he smiled at strangers, the way he could talk to anyone and seem at ease. As though failure and rejection were impossibilities. He was sure of himself. But it was more than mere confidence in self. It was as though he were sure about life itself, about its plan for him. As though his success was inevitable.* — Anita Kushwaha, *Bloodlines* [https://anitakushwaha.com/]

… green wiggly lines appear on the screen as the grammar app oh so kindly offers its "suggestions". The app wants us to insert "ands"; it complains about the incomplete sentences; it has a conniption fit.

If we were to obey the program and insert its desired ands and throw in a few semi-colons, tidy up Granny's word choices and shorten her sentences, the app would be quite pleased.

But the passages would lose all their power.

We must keep in mind that most writing programs/applications were *originally* devised to be used in offices for writing letters (e.g., Microsoft Word) to help secretaries spell things properly and for secretaries to be able to ensure no grammatical errors would embarrass their bosses.

Very quickly, "desktop publishing" came along and applications were massaged and the computer developed into having the capabilities for adding headers and footers, providing widow control, keeping footnotes where they belonged, making bibliographies and, blessed be, an easy-to-create index! "Books! We can do books now! Whole books!"

Your best bet would be to disengage your grammar app entirely [*See*, Appendix 2] and take a few (nay, several) courses in grammar and editing so you can learn how to do it right. This would involve some extra hours of work, but would save a lot of arguments with a mindless uncaring computer program.

The purpose of writing anything is to communicate your idea into another person's head. If a potential reader happens to purchase a book you wrote that they can't make hide nor tail of, you've not only lost *that* reader, but probably some of her friends as well. And even if you *do* learn how to do it properly in the future, that reader will still remember your name. As Granny might say: "Once the cat is out of the barn there's no telling how high the cow might jump over the fiddle."

If you want to communicate motivations and emotions, don't trust a robot to tell you how. Believe in YOURSELF!

But take them grammar lessons first, eh?

The Mysterious Comma

From Wikipedia: In the 3rd century BC, Aristophanes of Byzantium invented a system of single dots (*distinctiones*) that separated verses (colometry), and indicated the amount of breath needed to complete each fragment of text, when reading aloud. The different lengths were signified by a dot at the bottom, middle, or top of the line. For a short passage (a *komma*), a *media distinctio* dot was placed mid-level (·). This is the origin of the concept of a comma, although the name came to be used for the mark itself instead of the clause it separated. The mark used today is descended from a diagonal slash, or *virgula suspensiva* (/), used from the 13th to 17th centuries to represent a pause. The modern comma was first used by Aldus Manutius.

No doubt, these *distinctiones* were first used by speech writers to aid rulers wishing to make a good impression on their rulees. "*Veni, vidi, vici.*" — Julius Caesar [Note: In a previous chapter, I wrote about manipulating the reader. To re-demonstrate, I will make you look up the meaning of the words *veni, vidi, vici* by stating: If you like erotica, you might have a little fun by switching their order.]

Commas are no longer used as indications of when or when not to take a breath when reading; they are used to set off elements of a sentence. Well, that depends. With communication, everything depends, doesn't it?

If we are, indeed, writing a speech (or doing a reading from one of our works), then we may put in all the commas — the take-a-breath-here indicators — our little hearts desire.

But for written works, commas should be where *grammatically* required, not where *dramatically* required.

Now I could rhyme off a litany of grammar terms, or I could provide some examples.

Commas are little hooks that can lift a phrase/adverb/expression/clause out of a sentence and move it somewhere else; or they can insert a phrase into a sentence. We need one on each end of these phrases/adverbs/expressions/clauses. Picture the cables on a window-cleaner's platform. Take one away … *Kaboom!*

If a phrase/adverb/expression/clause starts a sentence, the other comma is implied as in:

, Arriving home from work, Bill was hungry.

, Neverthess, he didn't want to cook anything.

, Dammit, I thought there would be something to eat.

Whatever is *between two commas* can be removed without damaging the sentence. Reminder: A sentence has a subject, a verb, and [usually] an object. Example: Bill ate his soup. Subject: Bill; verb: ate; object: soup.

A sentence doesn't have to have an object, as in: Bill was hungry. Some verbs don't require an object because they are … just that way. ["An action verb with a direct object is transitive while an action verb with no direct object is intransitive. Some verbs, such as arrive, go, lie, sneeze, sit, and die, are always intransitive; it is impossible for a direct object to follow." www.chompchomp.com/terms/intransitiveverb]

Bill ate his soup.

My brother, Bill, ate his soup.

I could have written "My brother Bill ate his soup", but I have only one brother. Leaving the commas out in a case like this would imply that, perhaps, my brother Tom did not eat any soup. Spot the difference between "my brother, Bill" and "my brother Bill? The lowly little comma wields great power in the right hands, doesn't it?

In the sentence above, I am going to remove ", Bill," and this will give me:

My brother, Bill, ate his soup.

= My brother ate his soup. A complete sentence.

In my editing travels, I often see the comma appear only after the inserted name.
Let's remove the [erroneous] comma'd section from the following sentence.

, My brother Bill, ate his soup.

= Ate his soup. This is not a complete sentence.
Let's remove the implied comma'd section from this one:

"My wife Jeanne, my brother Bill, and the whole family went camping."

Oh, wait a minute. Looks like this guy has more than one wife and more than one brother … Hey! Come on. That's what is says right now. Fix by adding commas:

"My wife, Jeanne, my brother, Bill, and the whole family went camping."

No matter how cluttery it appears, the commas are needed to communicate the truth. If we are uncomfortable with all those commas in there, we can reword the sentence to avoid it.

"I asked my wife and my brother if they wanted to go camping. They said yes, so Jeanne, Bill and the whole family came to Bon Echo Park with me."

Note: I suggest we don't write: "I asked my wife and brother if they wanted to go camping." Best to write "my wife and *my* brother".

Commas for Which & That?

When do we use commas with these critters?

The lawnmower is broken. It is in the back yard.

The lawnmower, which is broken, is in the back yard.

What if there is a second lawnmower which is not broken? It is in the front yard.

The lawnmower that is broken is in the back yard. (The one that is not broken is in the front yard.)

Commas for Who & Where?

John lives in the park. In the park, there is a fountain.

In the park where John lives, there is a fountain. (This is about John.)

This is more about the fountain:

In the park, where John lives, there is a fountain.

Again, about John:

John, who lives in the park [or in a park — see the difference between "the" and "a" here?], is my cousin.

My cousin is John who lives in the park.

What happens if we write: "My cousin is John, who lives in the park." There is a subtle difference.

As there is between "John who lives in the park" and "John, who lives in the park." Can you feel it? The second one feels like it needs more information. Like a comma and the rest of the sentence perhaps?

Rather than regurgitate all uses of the comma, I'll supply a link: en.wikipedia.org/wiki/Comma You may trust what is written there.

Remain In-Tense — Verbs 1

Because verb tenses are so very important for communication, I am going to divide a chapter from *How to Write a Book: Park it, Get to Work* into two different chapters. (The whole chapter in one would be way too long. In fact, please forgive me for the length of this one. There was no good place to break it.)

Excerpt

Some languages do not use any more than three tenses: Past, Present, and Simple Future: I play, I played, I will play. English has twelve, with copious names for each (e.g., Future Progressive, Future Continuous, Simple Future Progressive, or Simple Future Continuous are all the same description for: "I will be playing."). And of course, there are the inevitable exceptions and extras. I won't get involved in lessons, but will comment on those errors or misuses I see most frequently. I don't even burden myself with memorizing the myriad names of tenses — so neither will I burden you — because understanding the concept makes tedious memory work unnecessary. If you wish to get into a deep study of the vagaries of English verb tenses, there's the ever-available Internet. (And once again, just because it's on the Internet doesn't make it correct.) I'll provide examples of where writers sometimes go wrong in their usage of past, present, future, coulda, woulda, and shoulda, had had, and would have had had I had the forethought, et cetera.

SIMPLE PRESENT

I play, you play, she/he/it plays, we play, they play

SIMPLE PRESENT CONTINUOUS

I am playing, you are playing, she/he/it is playing, we are playing, they are playing

The difference between the Simple Present and the Simple Present Continuous is probably better understood by first giving an example using the Past tense: I played there yesterday means one activity, over and done with. I was playing there yesterday can imply a meanwhile back at the ranch type thing:

I played with my bike in the park yesterday. Usually I play with it in my friend's yard.

I was playing with my bike when my friend arrived and invited me to go down town with him.

In the Present:

I play guitar.

I am playing my guitar [right now].

SIMPLE PAST

I played, you played, he/she/it played, we played, they played

SIMPLE PAST CONTINUOUS

I was playing, you were playing, she/he/it was playing, we were playing, they were playing

SIMPLE PAST PERFECT

I have played, you have played, he/she/it has played, we have played, they have played

"Have you ever played in the park, Joey?"

"Yes, Officer Jones. I have played in the park. I played there on Tuesday. And yesterday, while I was playing there, Frankie came by and asked if I wanted to go down town with him."

SIMPLE PAST PERFECT CONTINUOUS

I have been playing, you have been playing, he/she/it has been playing, we have been playing, they have been playing

"I see. Have you been playing in that park all summer?"

"No. I have been playing in that park for only three weeks."

PAST PERFECT

I had played, you had played, he/she/it had played, we had played, they had played

Almost all books are written in the Past tense, but we think we are reading in the present.

Had is further back than the Simple Past, so writers run across this tense all the time and many writers have difficulty with it.

> *(1) He locked up his bike before he went down town with Frankie.*
>
> *(2) He had locked up his bike before he went down town.*

What's the difference between examples (1) and (2)? In (1) the boy simply locked up his bike then went down town with Frankie. In (2), we are expecting a but, aren't we? "He had locked up his bike before he went down town, but somehow it got stolen anyway."

I'm sure we've used something like this in our stories:

> *"I got something to tell you, Frankie. Something serious," said Joey, adjusting the phone closer to his mouth so he could whisper, so he wouldn't be overheard by his mother. "It happened yesterday."*
>
> *Before Joey had left for the park the previous day, he had seen something from this very window. He had seen something that had told him it might not be wise to leave his bike unattended in the park anymore. He had seen a strange man lurking in the bushes near the bike lock-up.*

While we are writing in this further-back past, we need to use had all the time. This can become tedious for both writer and reader if it goes on too long.

It is acceptable — and in fact, recommended — that once we establish the further-back past, we switch to the Simple Past during our flashback. When our flashback nears completion, we gently nudge our reader to return to the further-back past, then on we go back to our story (in the Simple Past). Still with me?

Perhaps a show not tell:

> *"I got something to tell you, Frankie. Something serious," said Joey, adjusting the phone closer to his mouth so he could whisper, so he wouldn't be overheard by his mother. "It happened yesterday."*
>
> *Before Joey had left for the park the previous day, he had seen something from this very window. He had seen something that had told him it might not be wise to leave his bike unattended in the park anymore. He had seen a strange man lurking in the bushes near the bike lock-up.*
>
> *The man had been wearing dirty clothes. He was unshaven and his beard stretched almost to his belt. As Joey watched, the man reached out with a set of bolt cutters and cut through the chain holding a red Shimano to its post. Joey had been frightened, not so much by the man himself, but by what the man had done.*
>
> *Joey heard a noise outside his bedroom door. "Gotta go. It's Mom. Catch you later, Frankie."*

The reason you don't continue to use the Past Perfect the whole time you're back there is because it takes away the immediacy of the event you're writing about. The reader's mind remains distant from the events: "This went on in the past so I don't need to concern myself with it." You aren't drawing the reader into your world to experience what happened with Joey and Frankie and the strange man.

Note

When Joey is speaking, he says "yesterday". When the narrator is speaking, the narrator must not say "yesterday", but must say "the previous day". This is something I run across quite frequently. Making this mistake is actually a very good sign that the writer is in the moment or in his world which is exactly where he is supposed to be. Don't worry about this kind of thing during your 1st draft. It can wait until the 2nd or even 3rd go-through. Careful of ago and other un-timely expressions, too.

PAST PERFECT CONTINUOUS

I had been playing, you had been playing, he/she/it had been playing, we had been playing, they had been playing

Don't panic. This is the same as those Simple Past/Simple Past Continuous examples I gave you earlier, except it's one step further ago. Same thing for Future tenses.

Remain In-Tense — Verbs 2

In my editing travels, I haven't run across too many problems with simple future tenses.

Excerpt

SIMPLE FUTURE

> *I will play, you will play, he/she/it will play, they will play, we will play or I am going to play, you are going to play, he/she/it is going to play, we are going to play, they are going to play*

SIMPLE FUTURE CONTINUOUS

> *I will be playing, you will be playing, he/she/it will be playing, they will be playing, we will be playing*

For this one, think Mission Impossible:

> *"You will fly to the mid-Atlantic where you will jump from the plane into a boat which will be waiting for you. This message will self-destruct in ten seconds."*

SIMPLE FUTURE PERFECT

> *I will have played, you will have played, he/she/it will have played, they will have played, we will have played*

This is not unlike had. It's ago in the future.

"By the time your plane gets to the mid-Atlantic, they will have served breakfast."

By the time you get there, something will be over with.

But ...

Things can get a bit tricky when we "project" ourselves into the future while considering the past. Like this:

FUTURE PERFECT PROGRESSIVE

I will have been playing, you will have been playing, he/she/it will have been playing, they will have been playing, we will have been playing

"By the time your plane gets to the mid-Atlantic, the boat will have been waiting for one hour."

Once again, it's an ago, but an ongoing (continuous) ago. [Note: Don't ever use Canibus when you're trying to figure this stuff out.]

Here's a link that will give you a recap of all the verb tenses: http://www.teaching-esl-to-adults.com/verb-tense-list.html

THE WORLD OF IF

If it were done, when 'tis done, then 'twere well it were done quickly. — *MacBeth* (Act 1, Scene 7)

MacBeth is one of my favourite Shakespearean plays, and I think one of the reasons it's my favourite is because of this particular passage which still gives me the giggles.

Yeah. But isn't that just obscure Shakespearean Olde English talk? Nope. If I were to write it today, it would come out pretty much the same:

If it were done, then when it is done, it would be great if it were done quickly.

This is the **Subjunctive** tense — or Subjunctive mood as the aficionados like to call it. The following link explains the Subjunctive very well with clear examples.

https://englishplus.com/grammar/00000031.htm

They don't teach Latin in schools much and more's the pity (as the old wives say). The study of Latin gave me a clear understanding of the Future Pluperfect Subjunctive and its ilk. I enjoyed it. Translating Latin into English was to me like a code-breaking game. It was fun. (But then again, I was a bit of a nerdette.)

http://en.wikipedia.org/wiki/Subjunctive_mood#Perfect_and_pluperfect_subjunctives

Woulda, coulda, shoulda very often are incorrectly written as would of, could of, and should of — no doubt arising from the sound of the contractions would've, could've, and should've. The correct way to write them is: would have, could have, and should have, or, in the contracted forms. [But delightful in dialogue (for one character per book, though right?).]

> *I know I lead a busy life, but perhaps I should have spent more time with Roger before he took up with that woman. I would have if I could have.*

- Think of should as being guilt-inducing.
- Think of would as being polite, or possible, or somewhat willing with a "but" that goes along with it.
- Think of could as being able, with that same "but" attached.

All three of these are in the realm of the negative, the not real, the world of If.

If I were to take the time to write out several examples from this world of If, you might never forgive me.

End of Excerpt(s)

Oops! Dammit! & Other Exclamations

I have a potty mouth so I'm not doling out advice about restrictions on some of these words because I'm a prude or anything. You can trust me on that one.

Some genres tolerate cursing/swearing and expletives much more than others. Some genres (Victorian Romance, for example) have their own wonderful way of calling someone out without actually using any curse words or expletives. Good old subtext rides again!

I'm not a religious zealot either but I strongly suggest we restrict the use of the words Christ, Jesus, Allah, God, etc., when our characters are ranting. And never in narrative unless — there are always exceptions, aren't there? — the story is written in 1st Person and we *need* to show the narrator as having the type of personality who would use these words to express anger.

I see words in the following list being spelled in a variety of ways. In the … what one might call "the better publications" (Doubleday, Random House, Scribner, Viking, Bantam) … these are the spellings I have found to be most consistent across the board, and the meanings they convey.

Those with a non-English mother tongue will have come across variants but if we are writing in English with a North American English market target in mind, it's best to stick with North American English.

I have left out particularly offensive words from this list — but their meanings and some delightful ways to use them are accessible through a few links at the end of this chapter.

It's best we restrict our expletives to **one character per book** and this, with restraint. A group of gang members (secondary and tertiary characters) could use similar expletives/exclamations to portray the stereotypical gang mentality — blatting sheep — but once or twice only.

Once it's established that a character has a potty mouth, it's not necessary to continue showing it. We can treat this the same way we treat accents. Establish that a character *has* one, then structure the sentences afterwards to indicate the accent/cursing without actually writing it out.

Two characters who didn't grow up together or come from the same geographical area, most likely won't use the same expletives/exclamations — *the author's own, for example* — so we need to watch out for this.

If we must have one character swearing, we can always get creative with a secondary character, our Sidekick, for example. There are enough ways to show our Protagonist's anger/frustration/rage without resorting to expletives. I think we all remember having our mother, a spouse or a friend go silent on us. A spew of bad words is much easier to deal with. And as far as readers go, even I am offended if I'm required to wade through an overabundance of curse words.

agh: medium frustration
ah: often followed by: "I see …" as in: "Ah. So you don't have an alibi for that time slot. I see …"
aha: discovery
ahem: "excuse me"
argh: greater frustration
aw: isn't s/he/it cute; awe is a feeling of reverential respect mixed with fear or wonder
aww: what a kid would say as a complaint to a parent, "Aww. Do I have to?"
Christ: [a curse] avoid; but acceptable for one [male] character, once per book
christly: an adjective (despite the "ly"); preferably used only by one male character per book to describe something that's not working properly: "that christly dishwasher isn't emptying right again"; not generally to describe people (but could refer to "the neighbour's christly cat" or "that woman's christly dog"). [NOTE: Microsoft Word will insist on a capital letter but it should be lower case. In any case, it would not be "Christly" to describe a holy Christian, it would be Christ-like.]
crap: a euphemism for *shit* but still not in polite usage for female characters, although a female character can shoot craps (play dice); mostly used when a character is "sick and tired of putting up with his/her/their crap" and a totally fed up and angry female character could use it in this instance
cripes: euphemism for Christ; probably regional
cum: in reference to ejaculate or to the act of attaining organism, should be spelled *come* except when texting
dammit: I have seen this spelling much more often than *damnit*. Damnit in my view should really be written as "damn it" (two words) and which would then mean that whatever the "it" is, should be sent to whatever hell the character is referring to. Not the relatively innocent "Oh, dammit. I missed the bus."
damn: see *dammit*
damned: not dammed; rivers are dammed; it's sinners who are *damned* to hell/eternal damnation/etc.
dang: euphemism for damn, damned, dammit, damn it, etc. Usually used by elderly religious country folk
gee: euphemism for Jesus. It isn't spelled jee.
God/god: with the capital, signifies a named deity so should be used with respect. I recommend, for instance, if a character is using the OMG expression, that the writer types it out as "oh my god," rather than "oh my God" which would be closer to praying than to expressing shock.
god-awful: is an acceptable expression that does not offend [most] Christians or [most] other religions
goddammit: is the right way to spell this expression to use it in a mild form. If an exorcist were to use the

expression, it would be written as "God, damn it."

grrr: comedic frustration

ha ha: this is the correct way to spell a laugh, not haha

hah: variant of aha (see above) but with a slightly different meaning as it contains more contempt than joy of discovery. "Hah! I thought so, you rotten [expletive]. You were lying all along."

hardy har har: I would imagine that this term [today] would be used only within dialogue to mock another character sarcastically: "Well, hardy har har. Aren't we funny this morning."

harrumph: what a stuffy old man or woman back in the Victorian era would grunt to express his distaste

hee haw: this is the sound donkeys make

hee hee: this is a giggle

heh heh: this is not exactly a laugh. This is what a character would say — usually to him/herself — when s/he has just gotten away with something, or when planning to do something sneaky. Usually used comedically. Picture a cartoon villain twirling his moustache with a speech balloon over his head saying "Heh heh."

hem and haw: this isn't a dialogue expression. It's an actual term meaning to vacillate (be indecisive). Not to be used in place of "Hmm" or "Aha".

hip hip hooray: a cheer and this is how it's spelled. British spelling is often hoorah, but in North America, it sounds like hoo RAY, so needs to be spelled that way.

hmm: usually the first expression in a bit of dialogue as: "Hmm. Very interesting," or by itself to convey the same concept

ho hum: not used in dialogue to express fatigue or boredom; instead, it is used as an adjective to describe something: "The opening act was ho hum but we really enjoyed the main event."

howdy: usually in Westerns as a greeting

huh?: "What?" "What do you mean?" or without the question mark as: "Huh. I never thought of that ... Amazing."

I dunno: very informal in dialogue to mean *I don't know*

I wanna: very informal in dialogue to mean *I want to*

jeepers: see gee

jeez: see gee

Jesus: [a curse] avoid; but acceptable for one [male] character, once per book. (When I was a teenager, my elderly auntie overheard me use this word to express my anger. She took me aside and said, "Don't use Jesus as a swear word, Sherrill. 'Fuck' is ladylike. 'Jesus' is not.")

ma'am: how to spell it in cases like "Yes, ma'am."

mmm: usually the first expression in the sentence and means *pleasant*: "Mmm. This wine is lovely," or "Mmm. You're a good kisser."

nah: no. This is kind of a rude way of saying no. In a breakfast scene when Mom asks little Johnny if he wants strawberries on his cereal and he says "Nah," he's gonna get a good [figurative] slap.

naw: a misspelling of *nah*, above

nope: a stronger no than *nah*. Little Johnny will get a [figurative] slap if he uses this one on Mom, too. It's firmer than *nah*

num num/nom nom: "this gets my salivary glands operating" *num num* is the usual, but *nom nom* seems to be quite prevalent on social media. Suggest we stick with *num num*

oh oh: "That can't be good." See also, *uh oh*, below

OK/okay: I've seen it as okay. In fact, I used to think this was the correct way, but after seeing it so many times as *OK*, I just had to go check things out more thoroughly [by searching "origin of okay"]. OK is the original

oops/woops: *oops*, I've done something clumsy; *woops* is also used on occasion (mostly social media, so suspect); *whoops* are sounds, example: war whoops, but I've seen it (mostly on social media, so suspect)

ouch: that hurt

ow: that hurt more

shite: a cute, much less offensive way to say *shit*. My grandfather, who came from an Irish background, used to mention Skeever McShite to us grandkids on occasion, as though he were about to begin a story, but he never did. I have no idea who Skeever McShite was and Google doesn't either.

ta ta: bye bye; mostly British

tata: baby talk for thank you

tsk tsk: what a shame you did that; usually tsked by some older woman with her judgemental nose in the air; this is the way it is spelled

uh huh: yes; often absent-mindedly

uh uh: no

uh oh: that's not good! See also, *oh oh*, above

umm: give me a second to think about this; I don't quite understand; I'm thinking of some way to get out of what you just asked me to do and I'm letting you know that. *Hum* is what bees do; *humm* is not how to spell it, either

yay: hurray (not *yeah* which means yes)

yeah: informal *yes*

yee haw: cowboys say this and it can mean anything from *let's go* to *way to go, buddy!*

yep: one say of saying a very informal *yes*

yikes: caused by a sudden fright or by a sudden, unexpected injury but [usually] not an injury by anything larger than a bee stinger

yippee: a youthful way of saying *hooray*

yup: informal way of saying yes. Can contain happiness, full agreement, or sarcasm

The Scottish are exceptionally good with insults, cursing, and profanity [Warning! Extreme language even for me.]: https://www.youswear.com/index.asp?language=Scottish

In my opinion, however, nobody beats the Spanish. [Warning! Extreme language even for me.]: https://en.wikipedia.org/wiki/Spanish_profanity ; http://chromlea.com/spanish/swear-words-extreme.php

"That's a nice gift, Bobby, but I asked for a **SHIP** in a bottle."

Malapropisms — Say it Isn't So

From **WIKIPEDIA**, the free encyclopedia: *A **malapropism** (also called a **Dogberryism**) is the use of an incorrect word in place of a word with a similar sound (which is often a **paronym**), resulting in a nonsensical, often humorous utterance. An example is Yogi Berra's statement: "Texas has a lot of electrical votes," rather than "electoral votes". The word malapropism comes ultimately from the French* mal à propos *meaning "inappropriate" via "Mrs. Malaprop", a character in the Richard Brinsley Sheridan comedy* The Rivals *(1775) who habitually misused her words. Dogberryism comes from "Officer Dogberry", the name of a character in the William Shakespeare play* Much Ado About Nothing. *These are the two best-known fictional characters who made this kind of error — there are many other examples, such as Leo Gorcey's character "Slip" in* The Bowery Boys. *Malapropisms also occur as errors in natural speech. Malapropisms are often the subject of media attention, especially when made by politicians or other prominent individuals. The philosopher Donald Davidson has noted that malapropisms show the complex process through which the brain translates thoughts into language.*

What does it matter if we use a word that isn't exactly the ultimate, perfect, absolute match for what we're trying to say?

- we **confuse** the reader, therefore
- we **annoy** the reader
- it makes us look like we merely **ran off at the mouth** and let fly with whatever the hell came into our heads

- it makes us look too **cheap** — or maybe just **too damned superior?** — to hire an editor who would find and fix these errors for us
- it will make our readers **laugh at us** (or at worst, cry with frustration at having **wasted *x* number of dollars** on one of our books)

I would suggest that the only time an author should use a malapropism is in dialogue, for only one character per book, and in only one book per lifetime of that author (unless it's a series).

The following poem [thank you, Carol A. Stephen] sums up the evil of the malapropism in a delightful manner.

Reprehending the Meaning

We live in a doggie dog world where the early bird

gets to squirm, everyone striding to be first among sequels

starring the same old horse of a different collar, ridden with insecurity.

A glitch in time craves twine but forfeits weapons of mass production:

the whole wall of tacks. To the victim go the soils of spore,

yet the sun always sets on the blessed.

As sure as knight follows Dei, don't is a contraption beyond

my apprehension. In my Last will and tentacle, when I'm dead

from cardinal arrest and long years of very close veins, I bequeath

an expensive pendulum taken from the neck of a wolf in cheap clothing,

a man of carnival instinctuals unparalyzed in history since Michelangelo

painted the Sixteenth Chapel.

He was a man of great statue, headstrong as an allegory.

I have no delusions to the past. I have extra-century perception.

The hookeries and massageries turned the whole world

into Sodom and Glocca Morra, the flood damage so bad

they had to evaporate the city, creating dysentery among the ranks.

And still, a sudden thunderstorm wrecks havoc

in my garden of wood and weevil. Only the lettuce survives.

We dine on salad, sprinkled with some of those neutrons.

They crunch, but the sound falls on left years.

We are too long in the gravy.

August 5, 2015 © Carol A. Stephen

Similar to the malapropism is the use of creative flare to change a familiar **cliché** or to mix a **metaphor**. A character (one please!) could do this in dialogue to show his naïveté but we must not abuse clichés or metaphors in narrative.

Examples of **mixed metaphors**: http://www.jimcarlton.com/my_favorite_mixed_metaphors.htm

"Though you didn't actually attack the victim, your endlessly droning on about technical stuff did bore him to death."

Author Intrusion & Other Writing Crimes

Author Intrusion, to put it bluntly, is showing off one's own personal knowledge instead of the character's about what's going on in the scene. I used to breed and train show dogs [Rottweilers; and I owned and showed a Coton de Tuléar (a small, white, long-haired, sweet-natured, and funny dog)] so I have to really watch myself if I'm writing about a dog in a scene. I'm not this bad, at least I hope not — *no! I'm not!* — but it's a good example.

NOTE: The character, James, knows nothing about dogs. Doesn't own one, never did, doesn't even like them, and most certainly knows nothing about breeds or Breed Standards. Note also that we are in James's head; in his POV (Point Of View) so everything the reader sees is **supposed to be** through his eyes and his **knowledge base**.

James hadn't biked in this part of town for more than three years. As he approached the blonde in the tank top with the male Coton de Tuléar on the end of a Flexi (not a good choice as far as leashes go as dogs' necks can be injured if they run quickly to the end of it; people's hands can be injured, too, as they can get terrible burns if they grab the line, especially if their dog is fast), James decided he would make a note of the time and cycle by here again the next day in the hopes of seeing her again. He slowed down. The dog was a male because it was lifting its leg to urinate on the fence. It takes about twenty minutes a day to groom a Coton because of its long white hair that reaches right to the ground. The woman probably used grooming chalk on its muzzle as there was no tell-tale staining from food there. With its immaculate full coat, the dog was no doubt a show dog. As James stepped off his bike, the woman gave a command to the dog and it circled around to sit at her left hand side. The dog had been obedience trained well.

"She listens well, doesn't she? Is it a boy or a girl? I've never seen one of those. What's it mixed with?"

Have I lost you yet? Who cares if the dog's muzzle is stained or not. What has that got to do with anything in the story? James wants to get laid, that's all. He's not the least bit interested in this woman's dog except to find out if it will bite him if he gets too close to her.

Of course this is an extreme exaggeration, but we often do this without realizing it.

I'm getting lots of practice with this Author Intrusion business while I write my Kesk8a series. These books are written from the viewpoint of a Mi'gmaw woman (the series will stretch from 1681–1755 (from the advent of the Newcomers to Keskoua's neighbourhood to the Expulsion of the Acadians); she will age from 15 to 90 over this time period). The challenge for me is that she can describe anything because she's the narrator; but she can only describe what's in her own knowledge and experience. It's actually great fun being inside somebody's head and trying to see how she would see it. This is how she describes a violin in *Death in l'Acadie: a Kesk8a story*:

... Monsieur Petitpas knew a soldier from the fort who played what they called a fiddle: a beautiful shiny red-painted box with a womanly waist and strings from what would be her chin to where her legs would meet. He scraped a stick across this box to make sounds like a woman inside it was singing the highest notes possible. It made bumps on my skin to hear it. Later I saw that the stick had many fine threads from one end of it to another. Marguerite's cousin—her name was Antoinette—told me the threads were made of catgut but that the catgut was sheep guts. (I would never understand these people.)

Here's a bit more information on Author Intrusion: https://penandthepad.com/example-narrative-intrusion-1745.html

My Boss Is a Tyrant — 1

Notes to Self

- Sometimes I can't find the energy to write anything.
- I don't have time to write.
- I'll do it later.
- I'll start writing when I retire. I'll have lots of time then.
- I don't know how to get started.
- I wouldn't be any good anyway.

Excerpt from *How to Write a Book: Park it, Get to Work*

"Hints for Keeping at it"

It's a Job!

Whether or not you work from home, set aside the same two, three, or four days in a row each week for writing. If you make Mondays one of your days, then take Mondays off on long weekends. You must think of it as work, as a job, and not as something to do only when inspiration sneaks up behind you in the Ocean of

Creativity. You will soon discover that inspiration will come when *you* want it to, not randomly, like shark attacks.

Set the alarm to wake up by a certain time on those days. Give yourself only one hour to shower, eat, dress, etc. — the same as you would do for a regular job working for somebody else — then *get to work on time*. (I'm suggesting mornings because our Lizard Brain is probably still asleep.)

Take Breaks

When you're working, take regular coffee breaks. If you're in the middle of a thought, scribble a note, get back to it later. You'll be surprised at how well the brain learns and retains when it wants to. If a dog can understand the word cheese, spoken or spelled, in three different languages, surely we can retain a thought if we make a note.

It's not a good idea to write when we've consumed mind-altering substances like alcohol or drugs. These interfere with Muse communication. We need to set our hours around that activity if we indulge. Incidentally, almost all antidepressant medications throw cold water on creativity.

Keep Your Actual-Writing Work Day Short

Punch out after two or three hours of actual writing, but make it always the same time limit even if nothing seems to be going down on paper. The logic behind this is simple: You leave something when you are still in the middle of enjoying it, so human nature will make you anxious to get back to it. Or, if you're sitting there, not allowed to do anything but write, you might as well write. Right?

After you punch out, turn off your writing brain by doing something mindless for at least fifteen minutes. Something like *Forge of Empires*®, solitaire, or mahjongg. Think of this mindless activity as a decompression chamber for your right brain. [The right brain deals with concepts, the left with details — unless you're left handed, then it's opposite.]

Focus

During those two or three hours of actual writing, don't do anything else. Don't even answer the telephone. You're at work, right? Your boss is a despot.

You can make appointments on these working days you've chosen, but only in the afternoon, after work.

After Hours

On your working days, go ahead and make notes for yourself outside of your writing hours, but only up to a total of maybe seven hours all told. These outside hours are also a good time to do research but *relaxed* research — without pressure. Have fun with it. Then put everything away until next time. (Ah. Maybe your boss isn't such a despot, after all. See how lenient s/he is? See how you are loving this job already? See how spoiled you feel? See how anxious you are to get back at 'er next time?)

My Boss Is a Tyrant — 2

Notes to Self

- Sometimes I get frustrated and panic.
- When I panic, I can't concentrate.
- It's useless. I'm the furthest thing from a writer there is.
- It feels like I'm running around without getting anywhere.

Excerpt from *How to Write a Book: Park it, Get to Work*

Leave It Alone

Don't do any actual writing (for yourself) on the other days of the week. (Unless you get a brilliant idea in the middle of the night that you *must* write down! And since this is when your Muse can contact you best, listen! Make those morning notes! Your Muse has been busy while you slept.)

Don't Fuss over Stuff You Can Fix Later!

I know it's rude to scream, but DO NOT EDIT YOURSELF as you go along. If you can't think of the right word, type in the wrong one, or the same one, or just type [word]. Go ahead and call everything *very big* or toss in *some kind of tree* or have a million *justs* in your writing. Now is *not* when you should be worrying about all those *there wases*. This is only the first draft!

When we write, we get — or *should* get — into the space where our characters live, where we see and hear and feel and taste and smell what they see, hear, feel, taste, and smell. We should be right in there with them, inside their heads. In there, we are mostly in our right brain where concept and dreams run free. There are no "guard dogs". (I dislike using the word *should* but sometimes it's necessary.)

We need to let the story flow out of us as we perceive it, as our characters react to what we've thrown them into and to what they're throwing at each other. We need to record everything as fast as we can type. That's all we should to do at this stage. Our Muse contacts us through our right brain and there ain't no dictionary on that side, no grammar rules, only concept, so we don't need to go around thinking that what our Muse says is lasered into stone, that we have to get it right on the way out of us or the sky will fall. *No*. The Muse can only give us the *idea* and we can only describe the idea by using the concrete language tools (words, grammar, etc.) available in our left brain's databanks. Our Muse can't tell us anything using words we don't already know. (Didn't think you were that good, did you?)

Read It Later

Don't re-read it from the beginning every time you get back to it. If you must, then re-read the chapter or page or preceding paragraph. I hope I don't need to explain why, but I'll give you a hint: If you have only two hours to write and you're going to be re-reading 200 pages ...

Let it all go, relax with it, work in chunks until the very end. Then set it aside for a couple of weeks, go out and partay, partay, partay. Celebrate! You've just written a book!

Then after those couple of weeks go by, pick up Your Book and start to edit. You'll be surprised at how good it actually turned out to be. Sure, you've got some spellos, and some grammar mistakes, and you've used the word *just* an unbelievable number of times, but, hey. It's not too shabby at all.

Some Harsh Words for Die-Hards

I know some of you out there — purists — find it difficult writing on a computer and prefer to write everything out in longhand or to use a typewriter. Please refer to the section on The Lizard Brain [*See*, chapter De-Stressing] and stop doing that! It makes writing so much easier to be able to use the Search function for something you wrote, but can't quite remember where it was.

For example, you are on page 427 of your first draft and you need to reintroduce that woman on page ... *Uh. What page was she on? And what name did I use for her again?* I'm lucky to have a somewhat eidetic memory, but because of the writing process even that gift doesn't always help me find what I'm needing. When we write, our right-brain (concept side) takes over and we get into that world — some of us more deeply than others — and it might be impossible to remember exactly where we threw that minor character in with her all-so-vital one line. It's a great red herring to be able to waste our time re-reading our whole book looking for something, then finding mistakes that drive us to correct them and then seeing something else we could add to our story and "Hey! This part's really good. Did I write that?" You've lost your way. You aren't writing, you are editing. *Tsk. Tsk.* Naughty writer! Not yet! You have a book to finish!

When you have it on your computer, you need only CUT something out and PASTE it somewhere else if you want to rearrange what you've written. If you change your mind, you can click UNDO and what you just moved will go back to where it was. (Too bad rearranging furniture wasn't so easy.)

Get a computer. Learn to write with one. You'll save yourself hours of messing around with stuff other than writing. Fight The Lizard Brain's reluctance to do anything different. Things change. If they didn't, we'd still be twirling sticks in little piles of shavings every time we wanted to reheat something.

My Boss Is a Tyrant — 3

Notes to Self

- I want to write something really different but I'm afraid to.
- I have a great story in my head but I'm afraid of offending somebody.
- Nobody will like my book, I just know it.
- What if I get sued?
- What if.
- What if.
- What if.

Excerpt from *How to Write a Book: Park it, Get to Work*

Hunch over when You Write

Don't let anyone look over your shoulder when you're writing. I'm speaking figuratively, of course, and sometimes we don't realize that we have somebody there telling us: "Oh my gawd! You can't say THAT!" Yes you can. You can say *anything* you want. As long as it's *true*.

You can have a character say and believe that "water flows uphill", but as a writer, you can't say that, because it isn't true. You can have a character say and believe that "all black people can dance", but as a writer, you can't say that, because it isn't true. You can have a character say that "prepubescent children enjoy sex with adults", but as a writer, you can't say that, because it isn't true.

Always tell the truth. Whether They want to hear it or not.

It's Not about You

Don't think of writing as a selfish act, think of it as selfish not to do it. No matter how ridiculous your viewpoint or idea might seem to perhaps thousands of people — even millions! — at least one Earthling will get it and be glad you had the guts to say it. (Besides, if a million readers think your idea sucks, that's a million people who've read what you said. There's no such thing as bad press.)

Don't Talk Your Story to Death

Any time you talk your story to someone, you diminish it. You might even lose it entirely. Try not to fall into the pit of "and then my character is going to do this and then my other character is going to do that. Isn't that cool? And then …"

You have to shut your mouth and keep it shut until it comes out of your fingers on your next work shift when you're in your world. It's easy to get excited about new ideas, but remember those primitive amygdalae who share your brain with you and how bored they might get hearing the same story twice.

It Must Be Important

Something — and I hope even atheist writers will agree — is driving you to write, so it must be important. What if nobody had ever bothered to write the instructions on how to land a plane? There are plenty of books on how to get it up there to fly it, but what if only you knew how to get an airplane back onto solid ground? Selfish. Selfish.

Ah, such responsibilities have we who look out from Life's disco ball onto the Earth. When a bee returns to the hive with news of distant pollen, it dances instructions for its fellow bees: "Hang a left at the Murphy farm, then go up over that stupid pine tree the Wilsons stuck in the middle of their yard — why they did that I will *never* know! Then hang another left at the cucumber patch. They're not ready yet, probably a couple more days. You'll be able to pick up a wind current there and just ahead is the most fabulous clover …" Communication!

Primitive man did much the same when he (yes, he) returned from hunting expeditions. The wife and kids had been stuck at home gathering, so were anxious to hear about the exploits of the hunters — something different. Exciting events had taken place at home, too. Stories were exchanged. *Stories!*

The need and the desire to communicate are in our DNA, in our collective spirit. But they won't do any good unless we can get them out of *here* and into *there* where they can be seen, heard, and experienced by others.

"Sometimes when I'm stressed out, I just float here and watch them walk around."

De-Stressing

Notes to Self

- Watching people walk around. For a writer, that isn't as relaxing and mindless as it is for "normal" folk. It's work.
- A writing colleague on Facebook says he's taking a "break from writing" to work on a character's background. That's not a break. That's work.
- Learn not to feel guilty about doing "different" work. Like writing a poem instead of keeping on with that story, or drawing or colouring instead of writing at all.
- I think writers are always "on" — even in our sleep! I most certainly am. That's work.
- When I get a brainstorm in the middle of the night, I e-mail or text myself rather than turn on the lights hunting for paper and pencil. Even the light from the cell phone is not a really good thing but it doesn't wake me up as much as full-blown lights do. Sleep [*read*, dream] time is valuable. (btw, I set my cell phone to All Alerts Off from bedtime to wake-up time. I strongly recommend it.)

Excerpt from *How to Write a Book: Park it, Get to Work*

The Lizard Brain

The amygdalae (singular, amygdala) are two little guard dogs deep in our brain. When any semblance of a threat — real or imagined — appears, they react to protect us. But they are lazy guards and have convinced themselves that they must never, ever learn anything new, nor un-learn anything they already know, just in case. Well, bless their li'l ol' hearts for caring about us that much, but sometimes they can destroy us with their caring.

This part of the brain is not called The Lizard Brain for nothing, it's the remnant of our evolutionary switch from ocean to land, and deals, pretty much, with instinct and biochemistry, not logic. Would you trust a primitive fish to tell you how to run your life? Of course not, yet to argue with The Lizard Brain is extremely difficult, it is what tells us not to put our hand into the fire. It also tells us that we'd better not let anybody in on that controversial idea of ours or they might not like it — they might not like us. One negative experience in our past can inform our "guard dogs" that we dare not take a chance even if our idea might be the best thing that ever happened since the self-parking car. Just in case? Just in case we become rich and famous? Just in case our idea gets read in schools for years and years into the future? One single experience that is perceived by the amygdalae as a negative or frightening one, can do us in as far as ever writing anything of our own goes. But it's possible to get over it. Not easy, but possible.

The Lizard Brain has come under more intense study recently because it seems the amygdalae are involved in the fear response that triggers a type of emotional learning. Scientists have found that it's also involved in aggression and in pleasure (the twisted pleasure that aggression can arouse in some individuals), in depression, and also (possibly) in autism, sociopathy, and psychopathy.

My genre is horror, my medium screenwriting, so obviously, I love this stuff (I've been fascinated by aberrant psychology since childhood), but I'm not introducing The Lizard Brain to you because I find it a cool concept. The Lizard Brain is where Fear of Failure and Fear of Success can root in irretrievably deep. We writers tend to be a sensitive lot, and we also tend to be somewhat solitary, so the only place we're going to get any toughness and determination, not to mention support, is from nobody else but our own selves.

For information on The Lizard Brain start with these sample links:
http://sethgodin.typepad.com/seths_blog/2010/01/quieting-the-lizard-brain.html
http://www.instantbrainstorm.com/lizard_brain.html
http://en.wikipedia.org/wiki/Amygdala
http://www.wisegeek.com/what-is-the-amygdala.htm

Breaking our programming isn't easy, but it's doable.

Breaking Our Programming

Back in the early '70s, I joined a New Age group that saved my sanity. I won't go into any of the reasons for that — you'll need to wait for my down-near-the-bottom-of-my-pile autobiography to get the titillating details of my life. But I will share that the most important thing I learned (besides the discipline of vomiting my guts onto paper daily, aka "Doing My Writing") was the game of Breaking My Programming. It wasn't ever a real game at all but in order to get it by the "guard dogs", we had to look at it as though it were actually fun to do. (Trust me, it wasn't any fun at all once I got into the down and dirty of it, but it ended up being liberating to the point of euphoria because it put a pinch collar around the necks of those amygdalae puppies of mine.)

We all have things we cannot do, or that we must do. It's those damned "guard dogs"! Speaking of dogs, many years ago I took one of my Rottweilers to an obedience course taught by a canine behavioural specialist. For our first lesson, we all stood in a large circle in the gymnasium while the instructor gave us some basics.

The first basic she mentioned was that we would be repeating a command to a dog about 1000 times before he would learn it. He would need to be told "Sit" over and over until it connected that "Sit" meant to put his butt on the floor.

"Wow," we all oohed. "Imagine that. One thousand times, eh?"

So I was resolved to be patient with my Phedra as she learned her obedience commands, one by one, day by day, week by week.

However, one day it dawned on me that even though I had only said it once, and had even whispered it, she had responded to the word "cookie" immediately. She even picked up the concept of spelling. Imagine that! (Another of my dogs knew cheese in three different languages, and spelled. He was even starting to catch onto the differences between Cheddar and Brie.)

Isn't it interesting how all Nature's creatures learn through something they like? Through fun? That's the only way to break our programming: If you pretend it's fun, it's easier.

I used to smoke cigarettes and I always removed the foil bit from the right inside of the cigarette package first. No idea why. Maybe the "guard dogs" at work? Maybe it's because I'm right handed. Who knows? I thought it didn't matter, so for my first attempt at breaking my programming, I decided I would start by removing the foil bit from the left side of the cigarette package first for a change.

I had no idea how difficult doing that was going to be! The first couple of times, it was excruciating. I even beaded up a bit of the old perspiration on the brow there, silly me. But it got easier, and easier, and easier to do until it didn't matter which side I removed first. It wasn't one of those step-on-a-butterfly-disturb-a-star things after all. The sky didn't fall on my head! What a relief for this Chicken Little.

So onward I went looking for things that I could change about my habits that didn't really matter a lick. I think it was some of the most fun I've had in my life. The relief of being able to do something I had thought myself incapable of doing was enormous. Serotonin-producing relief. It was a high!

Try it yourself. Of course you'll need to maintain a sense of intelligent choice here. It's not a habit that we drive on the right hand side of the road in this country, it's so nobody gets maimed or killed. If you really want to test out driving on the left, go to England, rent a car, and play with it where it's legal. If you've never eaten broccoli, force yourself to eat a bite of it just for the hell of it. But use your head! Allergies have nothing to do with programming. Allergies are real and life-threatening. What I'm talking about here is doing things just because they aren't cookies.

The benefits of breaking one's programming are several. One of them is that we end up looking at things from another point of view — quite the necessity for writers, yes? You will now know for certain what broccoli tastes like. By breaking our programming, we also change the pathways between brain circuits, plowing new ones, perhaps staving off dementia. Once our brain starts to build new roadways, it seems to like doing it. And never fear, we have lots of room in there.

http://www.sciencedaily.com/releases/2009/11/091117161118.htm

As writers, we need to have the ability to look at things from several angles. Thinking of the disco ball [See next page], it's like being able to change places with each other. From my facet in the disco ball, and from my experience, I see that we need only wish it. Never stop learning. Never stop researching. Never stop listening. A lot of what I knew for sure when I was growing up is no longer valid. Some of it isn't even close.

(Earlier in *HtWaB*): "Life is a big disco ball (and yes, I'm that old) illuminating the dance floor of the universe with billions of facets, each of which looks out from the central whole from a slightly different angle and onto a slightly different scene. No one looks at anything exactly the same way as anyone else even though we are all made of the same stuff, are all connected, and our core common. The writers among us have this obsession to report back everything we see from our unique vantage point. Why? That's what we do. It comes from outside us and inside us and drives us to write."

I Don't Know How to Finish

I Can't Believe it!

I've written a book!

I've created people who ran around and did things, loved each other, hated each other, saved each other from danger. I love them ALL! Yesss!

But I can't seem to stop going back into their lives and "fixing" this and "fixing" that. Just in case.

In the chapter on Writer's Block, I wrote:

> *We need to choose one story/book/article and be faithful to it until the end. When we get to the inevitable end of it where we almost always find it difficult to bid it adieu, it is quite acceptable [read, recommended] to start an affair with another story/book/article as this will entice us to hurry and finish the original so we can play with the new one. This is human nature no matter how hard we try to suppress it.*

… and …

Summation of Writer's Block Advice

- plug your ears to the voices of friends, family, and your self-deprecating self

- hunch over the keyboard so no one can see what you are writing
- love the one you're with until it's time to say goodbye

Fixable?

There's a condition called OCD (Obsessive Compulsive Disorder) which cause the sufferer to follow certain patterns of behaviour. These patterns can range from extreme to mild: blinking three times with the left eye before pushing any elevator button while in a building with more than six floors; avoiding cracks in the sidewalk ("Step on a crack, break your mother's back"); having an unnecessary fear of germs and constantly washing one's hands; always doing things the exact same way ("and expecting different results"); going over and over and over a manuscript believing that it's inferior somehow and needs to be perfectly perfect.

As writers, we must not do this kind of thing to ourselves. Having OCD would be an enormous barrier to being a writer in the first place so let's assume, since we have actually finished our book (right?), that we are free of the extreme version (usually related to the physical brain rather than to the [self-]conditioned behaviour (OC<u>P</u>D)) and find out what's next.

What's Next?

- Type "THE END".
- Go through it to ensure that no subplot thread went off to Limbo unless this was the conclusion of that [one] subplot thread. Fix.
- Go through it (yes, again) for <u>each individual character's</u> dialogue to ensure that his/her voice is consistent throughout and sounds like no other character's voice. Fix.
- Edit it for spellos.
- Edit it for grammeros in <u>narrative</u>. Characters can have grammeros in <u>dialogue</u> and in fact, it's recommended. Example: A teenager might say "Me and her went to the concert" or "Me and Janice went to the concert" but I doubt if any teenager would say "She and I attended the concert." It sounds contrived. Don't overdo regionalisms but throw some in for <u>one</u> character. In narrative, we must write the grammatically correct "between you and me" but in dialogue, we can have a character say "between you and I" because that's the way a lot of people talk.
- Do a manuscript exchange (good ol' barter system) with another writer, preferably one who writes in another genre, to get feedback from somebody who knows how to make story/character/etc. suggestions <u>without holding back!</u>
- Stew about what this colleague has suggested. Pout as much as you want then either accept or reject some or all of the suggestions. Forgive your newfound and valuable friend.
- Seek out an editor (or two, or three): http://www.editors.ca/hire/definitions.html
- Say "buh-bye now" to your baby and send it to your editor(s).
- Forget about it entirely.
- Get going on your next project.

"Robert writes books for the hard of seeing."

Indie Publishing

Traditional Publishing vs. Indie Publishing

With the advent of the Personal Computer (the PC) came the downfall of the book industry in its at-the-time modern state.

I was a typesetter from the late '60s to the late '80s. The process from an author's mind to the final product, The Book, was long and involved. The author typed, retyped, used Wite-Out®, scissors and Scotch® tape to produce a physical manuscript. S/He made last-minute hand-written notes in the margins and sent it off to companies like the ones I worked for.

Using a CompuGraphic phototypesetting machine, people like me typed it. I worked on something like this for the first several years of my typesetting career.

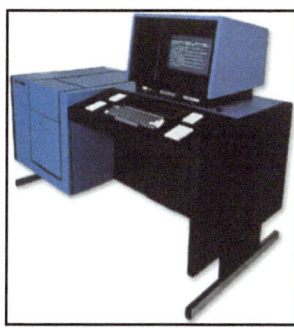

Things went to hell for most of us typesetters when the Personal Computer came along and secretaries could produce books for their bosses and have them come out looking like actual books. That was the end of me and my high-level salary. Off I went to the minimum wage level and a job as a receptionist at a busy veterinary clinic.

The Writers' Uprising

The Personal Computer allowed the writing spirit to rise up in almost every single person on the planet. I'd always been a writer, but working on everybody else's books had precluded my writing my own. I was stuck with writing articles, poetry and short stories. Who wants to type books all day — non-stop — then come home and type books all night?

Toward the end of my career, when I knew it was sliding into oblivion, I did write a horror novel, a great long beast of a thing, on a typewriter. Every day after work I would write several pages. Writing this beast kept me sane: I killed a grand total of twenty-six people in it. Violently. And with great pleasure.

Now I write on a computer where I can backspace, delete, cut and paste to my heart's content. I kill characters off but only when they deserve it and usually by their own hand (karma-wise speaking, that is) and often with humour (horror-fan humour). I don't have a gut need to write horror anymore; my life has stabilized, so I have expanded my horizons toward writing historical novels, crime, action/adventure, romance.

So what does all this have to do with Indie Publishing (once shamefully referred to as Vanity Press)? Everybody is writing a book these days. The original old time Traditional Publishers are overwhelmed with books, books, books in as many categories as there are authors.

Categories ...

Narrowed fields of interest = fewer sales. Traditional Publishers can't afford to spend all that time (*read*, money) working to produce a project like *Growing Rutabagas in Rankin Inlet* because the return on the investment required would be a negative one financially. TPs can take on only those projects that will appeal to the broadest range of readers (*read*, buyers). [Note: If *Growing Rutabagas in Rankin Inlet* were a Harlequin Romance and not a guide to gardening under almost impossible odds, then it might be a money-maker after all.]

As the book industry changed, the PC industry stepped in with all kinds of programs (thank you PC industry!) to help authors produce their own narrow-field-of-interest books.

Don't ever think that these narrow-field-of-interest books are of no value. They are of *great* value to their target readership. The next chapter will, I hope, give insight into how to produce one all by oneself.

"Productivity is up, but I miss my whip."

Do-It-Yourself Publishing

Offset Printing

Back in the days when I was typesetting, there was only one [modern] way to print a book. The process produced **galleys*** — long strips of photographic paper with "type" (set up in required font, point size, column width, etc.) — that the artists would trim, wax and paste onto perfectly measured and marked sheets of paper. These in turn would become photographic negatives that were "burned" onto thin metal plates which would be wrapped around the huge rollers on the printing press. This is called offset printing. A tedious process then, it's computerized now. The history of printing: https://en.wikipedia.org/wiki/Offset_printing

(I can't tell if this is one really huge offset printing press, or several. Must be several.)

Traditional Publishers use the offset printing process because it can handle quantity, and the quality is superior to digital. No need to go into further detail. Unless we plan to have thousands of units printed, we Indies don't need to know any more than what I've provided about offset printing.

Digital Printing

Almost all self-published/indie-published books are done *digitally*. Simplistically, this means toss it into a

---

*A woman I worked with back then would say, after our lunch or a break: "Well. Back to the galleys." Hence, this chapter's cartoon.

photocopier and push a button. Out comes a book. (Well, after collating, folding, trimming, and gluing on a cover, and other things happen, that is.)

What I will refer to as "Real [digital] Printers" charge a lot for a single copy of a book. so the trend is toward what is called Print on Demand, or POD. This means we won't have to take out a loan to get a single copy. The unit price is the same for one or a thousand copies.

There are a lot of companies who advertise POD services. Some of them are crooks so check around with colleagues before sending them any money.

I use a US company, Kindle Direct Publishing (https://kdp.amazon.com/en_US/) to upload my books to be available at Amazon.com (then subsequently to worldwide Amazons). They provide edit and design services as well (in US$). Because I do my own design, both interior and cover, I can't speak of the quality of their edit/design services, but I'm very satisfied with the quality of the books they produce.

An excellent company that colleagues are recommending is http://www.ingramspark.com/

Do-It-Yourself

Office 365: Microsoft Publisher

For those who have a knack for design, I can recommend Microsoft Publisher: https://products.office.com/en-ca/publisher. They have templates. They provide Help. I have Office 365 (I pay a monthly fee) and it comes with that app. Several apps are included with the Office 365 subscription. All good. But I don't use Publisher to design. https://products.office.com/ I use Word for writing and editing.

Serif

I use Serif PagePlus to design and have used it for years. I love it because it's typesetter friendly [*translate*, obedient]. There's a bit of a learning curve but once that has been surmounted, it's a delight to work with. Yes, they provide Help, as well. **_However!_** They have pretty much phased out that app into the equivalent of Adobe: Affinity Publisher and also Affinity Designer, both of which I need to learn [better]. This, I believe is a marketing ploy on their part so they can lure Apple users. Just sayin', eh?

Serif provides the PhotoPlus program, too, but have phased out toward their new Affinity Photo which I am learning to use and for some needs, now prefer over the well-known (to me) PhotoPlus program. My needs are basic so I haven't needed to get out my crampons, boots, ropes, pulleys and harnesses to explore *all* that Serif PhotoPlus offered by way of manipulating images, but I *definitely* need to learn something about interplanetary travel to learn Publisher and Designer (Moon height to me, this curve!) even though they provide workbooks. (I think they are assuming I know how to run Adobe. Not.) https://affinity.serif.com/en-us/

Adobe

I don't use Adobe so can't comment on it other than to say those who do, swear by it. I don't use Apple either, but those who do, swear by it.

Taming the e-Monster

Creating a project to upload as a print book is a relatively simple procedure:
1. design the book
2. save it as a PDF
3. upload it

An e-Book Is a Different Creature

What's the difference? A print book is a physical being; an e-book is a nebulous changeling whose form depends entirely on the e-reader it's downloaded into. The more-popular readers are Kindle, Kobo, and NOOK and the many distributors of e-books have their favourites.

Smashwords has a huge list of distributors: https://www.smashwords.com/about/how_to_publish_on_smashwords

E-readers vary in screen dimension and the material can be read either portrait-wise or landscape-wise. The size of the words can be varied as well. Pages and paragraphs flow so coding must be kept to a minimum. The nature of the beast demands it.

In order to upload an e-file to — let's use Smashwords as an example — it must be free of extra coding. Extra coding = junk.

The amount of junk that accumulates in a file is frightening. The only way to keep that particular monster at bay, is to give it a judicious cleaning. And yes, sorry to say, this requires work, attention to detail, a high "pain" threshold, and perhaps a sound-proof room (to keep little ears from learning naughty words).

Styles

Forgive me if I'm preaching to the choir, but I'm going to explain Styles anyway. Well, actually, I will direct you to Appendix 4 so you can learn about Styles on your own. What I will do is tell you why you need to learn how to use them.

I have only started using them within the last couple of years and after a climb up and over the learning curve, I can tell you that I absolutely adore Styles. When I am working in any document, I set up Styles for Title, Headings, Normal, Copyright Page, etc., and stick to them. That way, when I get to the design stage, I merely have to copy that particular file and save it as a .doc file. (This is important. It must be ".doc".)

All right. Now we have a .doc file with every single word in it tucked nicely into its own Style.

Now you must remove all the extra returns between everything. Everything! (Search for ^p^p and Replace with ^p. Do that until the little screen tells you 0.)

(By the way … I don't know how else to tell you this, so I'll just come right out with it: Any graphics or photos must be inserted later so make notes where they go. And keep in mind your Styles. Isn't this fun?)

Save!

Now Save As a **Web Page, Filtered (*.htm, *.html)**. Then close.

I came across a free ePUB creator that has reams of directions. Sigil: http://sigil.en.softonic.com/ At first it will be daunting but it beats paying somebody several hundred dollars if you can learn to do it yourself. Read all their Help files.

Open the Sigil program. From within the program, open your .htm(l) file and follow the directions. Check out the user guide. I wasn't kidding when I said "daunting", was I?

Once you have the file set up according to the Sigil program's desires, Save it.

Validate. Validate Validate.

I have also been able to find ePUB validators: http://validator.idpf.org/, https://www.epubconversion.com/epub-validator/, and https://www.ebookit.com/tools/bp/Bo/eBookIt/epub-validator. Use these before you even *think* of attempting to upload your ePUB file anywhere because those companies will reject your file if there is the slightest bit of non-Style in it.

There is nothing that fills my heart with more joy than having one of these validator programs come back with the message: No Errors Found.

So if you like a challenge, have a sound-proof room (believe me, even if you have never said more than "Oh poo" in your whole life, you'll be making the air blue taming this monster), then go for it.

When Do My Millions Start Rolling In?

Filthy Rich or Rolling in It?

Self-publishing rarely brings in millions of dollars. With Traditional Publishing, bringing in millions is rare as well, but we have a better chance at it.

Then Increase the Odds

Back when I was editing, to a [wo]man, a first-time author would exclaim after the editing process was over: "Thanks be! That was really hard."

I would reply with: "To that comment, I always reply with: ha ha ha ha ha ha ha ha ha ha ha Just wait."

In order to get even a toe onto the threshold of almost every Traditional Publisher (TP), we need an agent.

In order to get an agent to consider anything we write, we must impress the bejeepers out of her/him.

The October 2015 issue of *Writer's Digest* contains several articles on approaching, dealing with, and getting — <u>seducing?</u> — an agent. (The first step in seduction is to convince the other party that we have something they desire beyond all desires — whether they do or not. [insert winking emoji])

This means we have to send an agent the very best we can come up with so s/he can brag about us, excite the TP about our project. The best? Edited, edited, edited, then professionally edited; submitted using the standard MS format (12 point type, Times Roman font, double spaced, etc. — *or* whatever that particular agent's guidelines ask for).

Know the Rules

It's vital that we check out each agent's guidelines before we contact her/him the first time. Why before the first time? Aren't we calling her/him to find out what s/he wants us to send?

Tsk, tsk. Lazy, lazy! What if we phone the agent on a Monday morning and her online guidelines specifically point out that she takes phone calls on Tuesdays only? Or not at all?

Oops.

Agents don't want to handle clients who are too lazy to do the work themselves. An agent's job is to convince the TP to take us on. If our agent tells the TP: "Well, my client is busy with this and that, eh? She doesn't have time to do all that fussy stuff," what do you think the TP will say?

How Much Are these Potential Millions Worth to Me?

It's not a matter of waving a magic wand and turning our pumpkin into a best seller. We have to learn how to build our own carriage in the first place and apply our absolute best attention to every detail to turn that pumpkin into a valuable, jewel-encrusted carriage — without costing the TP anything extra (like hiring more editors, especially).

We also have to learn how to not only design what a TP would wish for, but convince our Fairy Godmother that our particular carriage is *exactly* what any given TP would wish for. This will help our agent seduce the TP into buying it. (Yes, you're hearing me correctly. We must pimp our projects, convince others to part with their money in order to have what they believe they desire beyond all desires.)

But we are the one who has to do all the work:
- research the market for our particular genre/format;
- ensure that our project will cost a TP next to nothing to produce it (i.e., it's been edited to the nth degree; set up in the proper format for publication (US or Canadian style, e.g.); most likely these days, be e-mail-able;
- and so on.

Always read the guidelines provided by every agent, every TP, every genre, every format.

From our side of things, it takes work not wishes.

I'm Ready for my Close-Up, Mr DeMille

Dealing with:

- the weirdness of having people look up to you now that you've published something — or won something
- nobody showing up at signings or whatever
- a ton of people showing up at signings or whatever
- being an introvert and having to behave like an extrovert (without having a nervous breakdown)
- having fans (They all aren't stalkers, you know.)
- talking about ourselves with confidence and without holding back (Here's a link about humility and self-confidence: http://www.chabad.org/parshah/article_cdo/aid/475512/jewish/Humility-vs-Low-Self-Confidence.htm)
- spending more and more time in the public eye

We can publish and have perhaps ten copies printed and leave them at home under the bed and never tell anyone about them. That would solve all of the above issues neatly.

But.

Deep down, I think we want everybody in the world to read our book(s). If this happens, we will become "famous" so will be forced to face our fears.

Each of us is an individual so there are no hard and fast rules explaining how to deal with these "problems" that we writers — shy folks for the most part — will eventually face once we publish.

The only way to deal with all of this is to deal with it internally, on our own individual terms, and one step at a time even though it's terrifying. In my post on "De-Stressing" I wrote about <u>Breaking Our Programming</u>. A writing colleague and I have been challenging each other to do just that. It's exhilarating! Actually fun!

"Guess what I did this week that I never did before! *Giggle.*"

"What?"

"I sent a story to a publisher. *Giggle.*"

"Aaah! You didn't!"

"Yes. I did. I really did. And I didn't have a heart attack or anything! And they even rejected it and it didn't make me want to commit suicide or anything."

"No kidding. You're an inspiration. I guess rejection isn't as bad as we imagine it to be, is it?"

"We're writers. Our imaginations work overtime constantly."

"So did they say anything about it?"

"Yes. They said I might consider changing the ending and then re-submit."

"What? That wasn't a rejection then."

"Oh. No. I suppose it wasn't. Imagine that …"

"How does it feel?"

"Uh. Weird. It makes me want to … to giggle."

"I think that's what happy feels like. Ya think?"

"Yeah. Maybe."

"I'm gonna give it a try but I'm scared out of my mind."

"Of what? What are you scared of?"

"Um. Huh. To tell you the truth, I don't really know."

"The Last Post"

Farewell. Adieu. Ciao. Adios. Auf Wiedersehen.

Yes. This is my final Post [chapter] for *Transplanted Heads: Your Muse Can't Write Worth Sh*t*. It's been a wonderful year and I've enjoyed sharing what I learned over the years.

Much of what I shared I learned through attending the meetings and workshops of Canadian Authors Association – National Capital Region Branch. (That's Ottawa.) http://canadianauthors.org/national/

I also learned a tremendous amount about writing when editing other writers' projects at http://crowecreations.ca/ (yes, that's me). Why did I stop editing? I apprenticed for twenty years as a typesetter (1969–88) so am very much qualified to edit right down to the nit-picky em and en dashes and to which side the quotation marks go around punctuation or whether or not the comma should stay in italics after an italicized word or not (US or Canadian style), et cetera. So when I edited a job, I edited from the heights to the depths of it. It was extremely time-consuming. But I am grateful for every un-apostrophed gerund I ran across. There is no benefit without sweat, is there?

I'm a nerdette. I Google everything. I question everything. I study everything. I enjoy everything. Follow my lead and you will learn an amazing amount about life (characters) and living (action). Read and study the methods required to get that life and living into readers' heads.

An excellent source for books about writing is *Writer's Digest* magazine. Awesome, awesome information in that publication! http://www.writersdigest.com/magazine

I have a bookcase full of how-to-write-whatever books that I acquired from *Writer's Digest* and devoured years ago. Most of these books are still available and can be purchased from Amazon. Is there anything that can NOT be purchased from Amazon?

Why?

Through *Transplanted Heads* I've covered most of what I know well from my own experiences. It is not in my nature to "wing" something I don't know well, so maybe I'll be back in ten years or so when I learn a lot more about writing/editing/publishing/marketing, etc. (Here I am five years later — having learned more — putting my blog into book format.)

I have a huge To-Do Pile and I am now in my mid-70s so it's not like I have sixty years left. I have only about half that. (I have good DNA on both sides, so there's hope.) I have published the second book in my *a Kesk8a story* series and I'm halfway through book #3. Six books are planned for this series. I have several screenplays to finish/start/write. More poetry books. See "About the Author" for my publishing credits.

Thank You

Through *Transplanted Heads: Your Muse Can't Write Worth Sh*t*, I've connected with a myriad of talented colleagues. Thank you for following me, for reading my Posts, and for being who you are.

Final Word

Dig deep and get it all out of you and onto the paper or the computer screen. The more you share of your own experiences, the better the opportunity to help someone else over the rough spots of life.

"Maybe we don't write very well. Maybe our language skills are not the best. Maybe we've been criticized for offending someone, for writing nonsense, for not writing within the parameters of The Box. That's not what's important. What's important is reporting what we see from our own perspective. Even if — through this reporting of our own experiences — we benefit only one other Earthling in our lifetime, that's enough. Those of us who are driven to write have a great responsibility indeed. This responsibility is so important, that if *we* don't grab the dream snippet *our* Muse gives us from the Idea Pool, someone else's Muse will snag it, hand it over to *its* writer who'll use it, and we'll miss out on the opportunity. Something that important can't be allowed to drift away into the ozone like some child's party balloon." — Sherrill Wark, from *How to Write a Book: Park it, Get to Work.*

> *It always helps if you put your fears out on the blanket in front of you so you can see them for what they really are.* — Keskoua, *Refuge in l'Acadie: a Kesk8a story* by Sherrill Wark

About the Author

Sherrill Wark is a novelist, screenwriter, short story writer, poet, book designer, former editor, not-so-little ol' lady but is otherwise normal. She's a member of CAA–NCR (Canadian Authors Association – National Capital Region branch) and is the former editor/designer of their e-mag, *Byline*. She is writing a series of historical novels about the Acadian people written from the point of view of Keskoua, a Mi'gmaw woman, and set in Port Royal, Acadia (Annapolis Royal NS): *Death in l'Acadie*; *Refuge in l'Acadie*; *Trapped in l'Acadie*; *The Hanging*; *The Cleansing*; and *The Expulsion*. And she sings soprano secundi in an Italian choir and kills people off in her dark short stories under a pseudonym.

Sherrill Wark is the author of:
Graven Images (horror, fiction)
How to Write a Book: Park it, Get to Work (non-fiction)
Death in l'Acadie: a Kesk8a story (historical fiction)
Refuge in l'Acadie: a Kesk8a story (historical fiction)
Vivie Goes to Hell in a Hatchback (YA, Action/Adventure, fiction)
The Closet Hides a Flight of Stairs (poetry)

As Christina Crowe:
A Girl Dog's Breakfast, scary stories and rude poems (fiction)
The Unkindest Cut: Short Creepy Movie Scripts (short creepy movie scripts)
My Search for Serotonin: Experiences of Suicidal Depression and How to Deal with it (self-help)

Appendix 1
Photo/Graphics/Cartoon Credits by Chapter

Muse? What's a Muse?, Moreau, Gustave Hésiode et la Muse - 1891
The Importance of Keeping Secrets, MB900111472
I Don't Know How to Start, Cartoon Stock, Cartoonist Chris Grosz, Search ID cgr0443
Naming Our Characters: Part 1, MH900445039
Naming Our Characters: Part 2, MH900432169
Naming Our Characters: Part 3, MH900057410
Let's Get Started, Cartoon Stock, Cartoonist Fran, Search ID forn602
Genre = Species, Cartoon Stock, Cartoonist Dave Carpenter, Search ID dcrn537
Story Structure, Cartoon Stock, Cartoonist Chris Madden, Search ID cman361
Surprise! Surprise!, Cartoon Stock, Cartoonist Kieran Meehan, Search ID kmhn206
Leaving Bread Crumbs, Cartoon Stock, Cartoonist Guy & Rodd, Search ID gra050506
No Loose Threads, Cartoon Stock, Cartoonist Tony Zuvela, Search ID tzun1197
Develop Laryngitis — Use the Right Voice, unknown source
Don't Stalk Your Characters, Cartoon Stock, Cartoonist Scott Hilburn, Search ID shl080716
Dialogue Maketh the Character, motorcycle from Word
The TV Brain = Talking Heads, 35688388_thumbnail
How to Get Away With Switching POVs, iStock_000007920649_Large
Subtext — Talkin' Dirty, Cartoon Stock, Cartoonist Scott Nickel, Search ID snin259

Making a Character Loveable, iStock_000026939005_Full
Making a Character Killable, iStock_000007600775_Large
Make 'em Wanna — Motivation, public domain
Conflict is Required, Cartoon Stock, Cartoonist Dave Whamond, Search ID dwh110405
Dilemma = Motivation = Story!, Cartoon Stock, Cartoonist Mark Guthrie, Search ID mgtn261
Go Ahead — Manipulate Your Readers, public domain
Be Kind to Your Critters, Cartoon Stock, Cartoonist Dan Reynolds, Search ID dren195
Yes, We Can Be Too Nice, Cartoon Stock, Cartoonist Jon Carter, Search ID jcen628
An Opinion for EVERY Character, Cartoon Stock, Cartoonist Kieran Meehan, Search ID kmhn749
Don't Muzzle Your Characters, Cartoon Stock, Cartoonist Bradford Veley, Search ID bven173
Using Backstory without Using It, Cartoon Stock, Cartoonist Huw Aaron, Search ID haan162
Describe without Details, Cartoon Stock, Cartoonist John McPherson, Search ID jmp050809
Describe through Action, Cartoon Stock, Cartoonist Chris Wildt, Search ID cwln3939
Blame it on Writer's Block, Cartoon Stock, Cartoonist Mike Baldwinn, Search ID mban979
Two Books in One?, Cartoon Stock, Cartoonist Fran, Search ID forn2130
Not Enough Novel for a Novel?, Cartoon Stock, Cartoonist Dominique Deckmyn, Search ID dden51
Too Many Cooks, Cartoon Stock, Cartoonist Will Dawbarn, Search ID wda0507
Recycling Characters, Cartoon Stock, Cartoonist Mark Lynch, Search ID mlyn1655
Making Your Grammar App Weep, public domain
The Mysterious Comma, Cartoon Stock, Cartoonist Jorodo, Search ID jdon260
Remain In-Tense — Verbs 1, iStock
Remain In-Tense — Verbs 2, iStock
Oops! Dammit! & Other Exclamations, Cartoon Stock, Cartoonist Dan Reynolds, Search ID dre1890
Malapropisms — Say it Isn't So, Cartoon Stock, Cartoonist Dan Reynolds, Search ID dren510
Author Intrusion & Other Writing Crimes, Cartoon Stock, Cartoonist Larry Lambert, Search ID llan547
My Boss Is a Tyrant 1, Cartoon Stock, Cartoonist Mike Flanagan, Search ID mfln6158
My Boss Is a Tyrant 2, Cartoon Stock, Cartoonist Stik, Search ID bgrn2738
My Boss Is a Tyrant 3, Cartoon Stock, Cartoonist Mike Baldwin, Search ID mban2446
De-Stressing, Cartoon Stock, Cartoonist Tim Thomson, Search ID tton135
I Don't Know How to Finish, Cartoon Stock, Cartoonist Kelly Kincaid, Search ID kkin31
Indie Publishing, Cartoon Stock, Cartoonist Naf, Search ID amc0401
1. Compugraphic machine, prepress_history_editwriter7500
Do-It-Yourself Publishing, Cartoonist Jim Sizemore, Search ID jsin39
2. offset printing press, unknown source
Taming the e-Monster, Cartoon Stock, Cartoonist Glenn and Gary McCoy, Search ID ggm071024
When Do My Millions Start Rolling In?, Cartoon Stock, Cartoonist Dan Reynolds, Search ID dre0350
I'm Ready for my Close-Up, Mr DeMille, Cartoon Stock, Cartoonist Mike Gruhn, Search ID mgrn420
"The Last Post", Cartoon Stock, Cartoonist Karsten Schley, Search ID kscn4336

Appendix 2: How to Disengage Microsoft Word's I'm-Only-Trying-to-Be-Helpful App

I use Microsoft Word because I like it for writing and for editing. (Apple is loved by many. I'm used to Word.) When Crowe Creations (me) gets a manuscript in for design, we are receiving *their* Microsoft Word copy which has [probably] not been modified to eliminate automatic set-up for standard business style. (Manuscripts are very different from letters to clients or business associates.) So I make the following alterations to a *copy* of their submitted MS. I keep the original, just in case, until it's not needed anymore.

So, how do I get it to calm down and point out only what I want it to?

Language

First, let's tell it what language we want it to use. If it's a full MS (manuscript), we need to highlight everything from beginning to end. (Place the cursor at the beginning of the text, then holding down the Shift key, hit the Page Down key until we get to the very end, all 400 pages if necessary.

Across the top of the Document "page", is a list: File, Home, Insert, Design, Layout, References, Mailings, Review, View, Help, Acrobat.

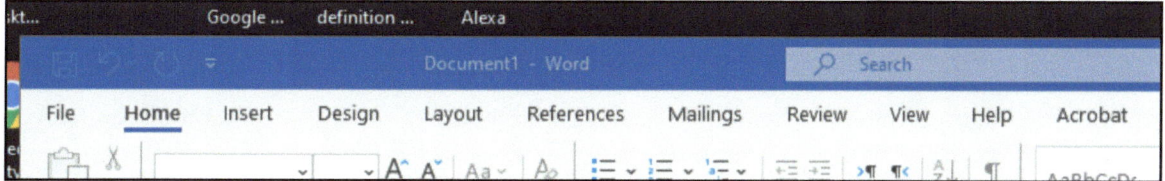

Place the cursor on "Review" then left click. Then click on the little wee down-pointing arrow under Language. Two choices appear. Click on Set Proofing Language…

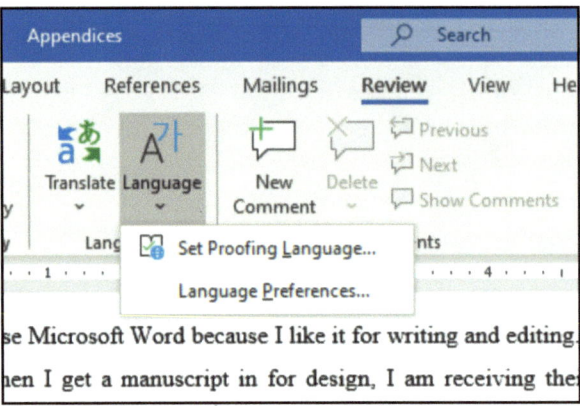

Something like the list below will come up. I am writing this in "Canadian" so that's why it says English (Canada). Incidentally, if you are undecided whether to write a MS (manuscript) in Canadian or US Style (*How to Write a Book: Park It, Get to Work* shows the differences in the chapter, "Communication"), write in Canadian style first. It is easy to Search/Replace (Appendix 3) from Canadian to American but almost impossible to perform the converse. It isn't just spelling. It's a lot of nerd/ette stuff. The spelling is not so difficult to change, it's the placement of the quotation marks, plus various other tiny differences — one tiny difference, I must confess, I ignore, but I'll never tell anybody which one.

Please note the two boxes near the bottom of the above cut-out. If you want to ignore spelling and grammar suggestions completely (not recommended), you may add a tick to the Do not check spelling or grammar box. Usually by the time we get to chapter 10 or so, it throws up its hands with the excuse "Too many errors" anyway, so we get a reprieve.

If we are going back and forth between/among languages, we could click on the Detect language automatically box, but I don't recommend it. We can apply a Style instead. (See Appendix 4 for Styles.)

Click on the language you want — it will be highlighted as it shows above— then click OK.

Automatic Changes

I have set my Microsoft Word app up to perform a very select few automatic as-we-type corrections. Example: Ever since my typesetting days, I've had a problem with typing two capital letters at the beginning of some capitalized words. Depends on the combination of letters. I used to think it was because I typed too fast, but since I'm slowing down — combination of old age, sore fingers and cheap keyboards these days — and I'm still doing it, I guess it's just me. I do appreciate being helped out with this one, but I don't want it assuming much else. Another example: It's considered old fashioned — and has been since I was typesetting (career bombed out in 1989) — to use superscript for numbered items, e.g., 2nd. It should be 2nd (or avoided altogether). But that's the editor in me so we can ignore that until our fifteenth draft if we wish.

Click on File.

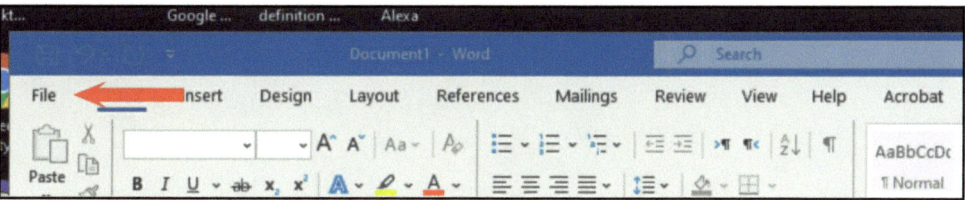

This will show up.

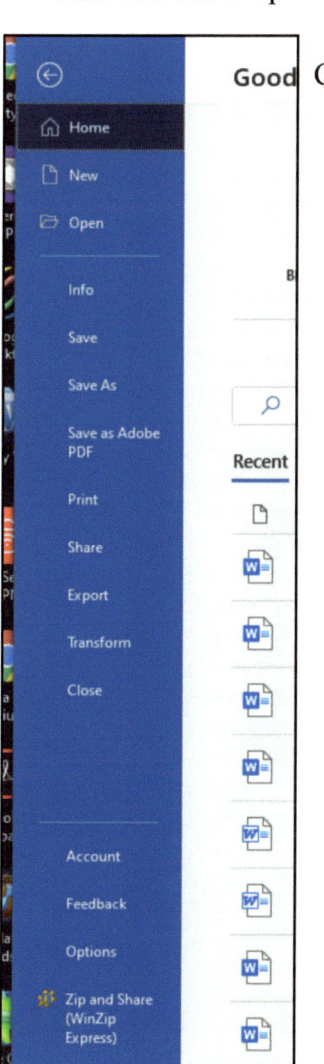

Click on Options (down near the bottom).

This will show up.

What I did when I first came across this seemingly bottomless pit of decisions, was go through it all, one section, one step at a time, and tell it what I wanted and what I didn't want.

Example: I set it up so when I hit hyphen hyphen, it will give me an em dash, regardless. (Microsoft is set up to give an en dash when space hyphen hyphen space is struck, and an em dash only when no spaces are on either side. This is US Style, now "being imposed on all other Em Dash Cultures around the world" complains Sherrill Wark, the purist Canadian, em-dash-lovin' nerdette.

I recommend playing with it but while using a fake file.

Appendix 3: Search/Replace

I'll go through this one as though it's a brand new concept.

I mentioned changing the name Frank to the name Ernest in the chapter, "Naming Our Characters: Part 1".

Click on the little arrow pointing down beside Find.

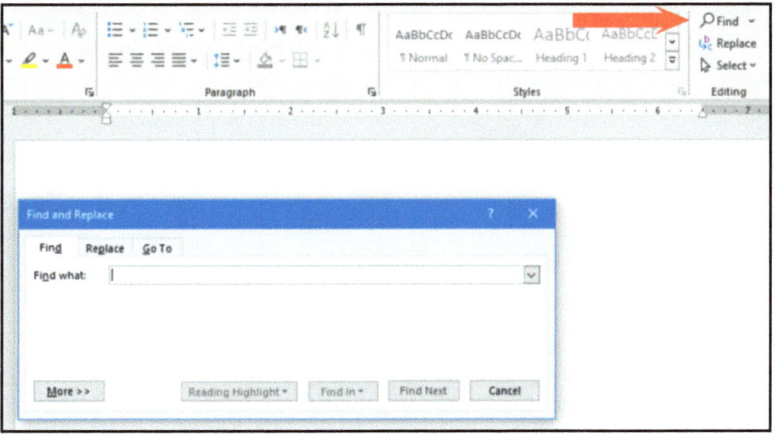

Click Advanced Find.

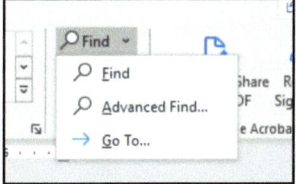

We can do these changes one at a time by selecting Find Next each time, then Replace (not Replace All, just plain Replace), until we get to the end of the MS.

If we are confident, we can click Replace All and like magic, everything will change instantly.

But before we do any of that, we need to click on the box that says MORE >>

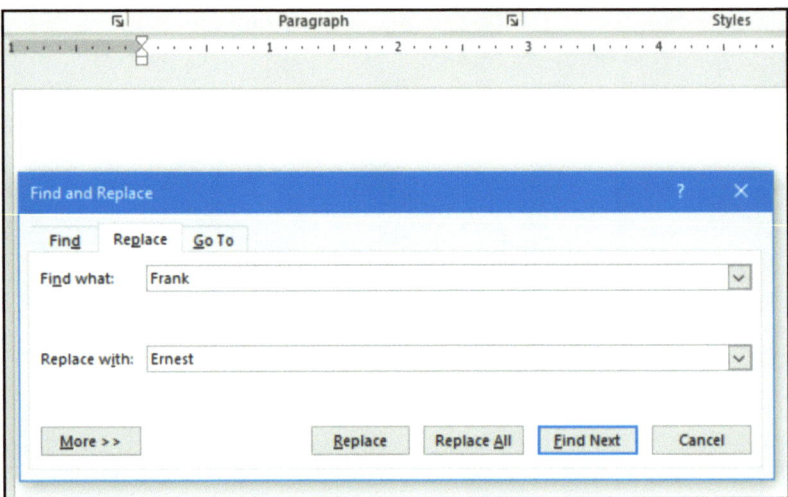

There, we will see several boxes.

For changing something like Frank to Ernest, tick the box that says Match case. And also tick the box over on the right that says Match suffix (to avoid Frankly and its ilk). Note: We need to get into the habit of un-ticking these things after each individual Search/Replace.

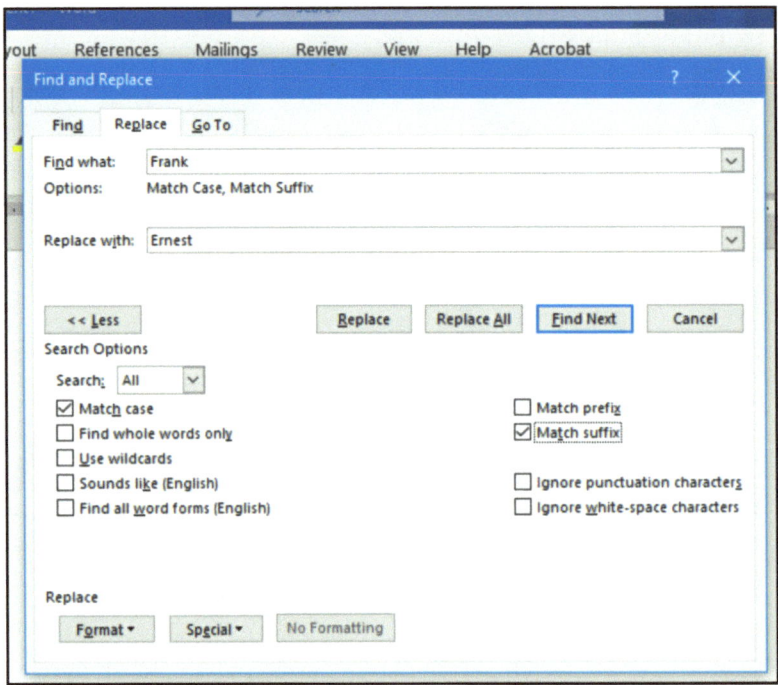

Now we can click Replace All with confidence.

Kapow. Done.

We can also change various characters like en dashes to em dashes, or remove tabs entirely when we want to submit our MS to our editor, agent or potential publisher. Click on the Special box (toward the bottom of this cut-out) and these will pop up.

I hope they are pretty much self-explanatory. We can always set up a fake MS file and play with them to see what all these do. But we need to remember to un-tick Match case and Match suffix and anything else we may have ticked, like I haven't done here.

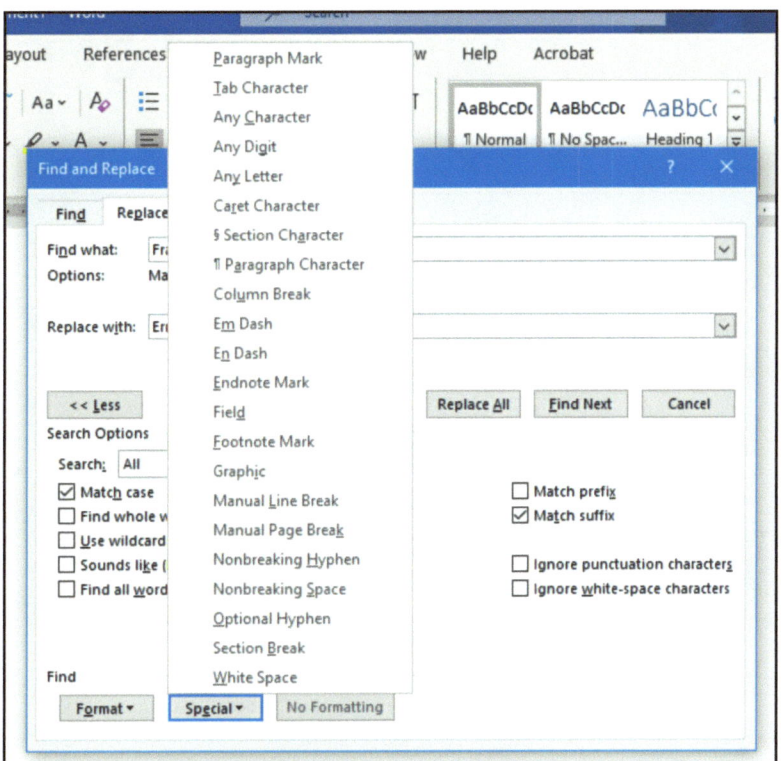

Appendix 4: Styles! The Most Amazing Assistant Ever!

So … What are Styles, exactly anyway?

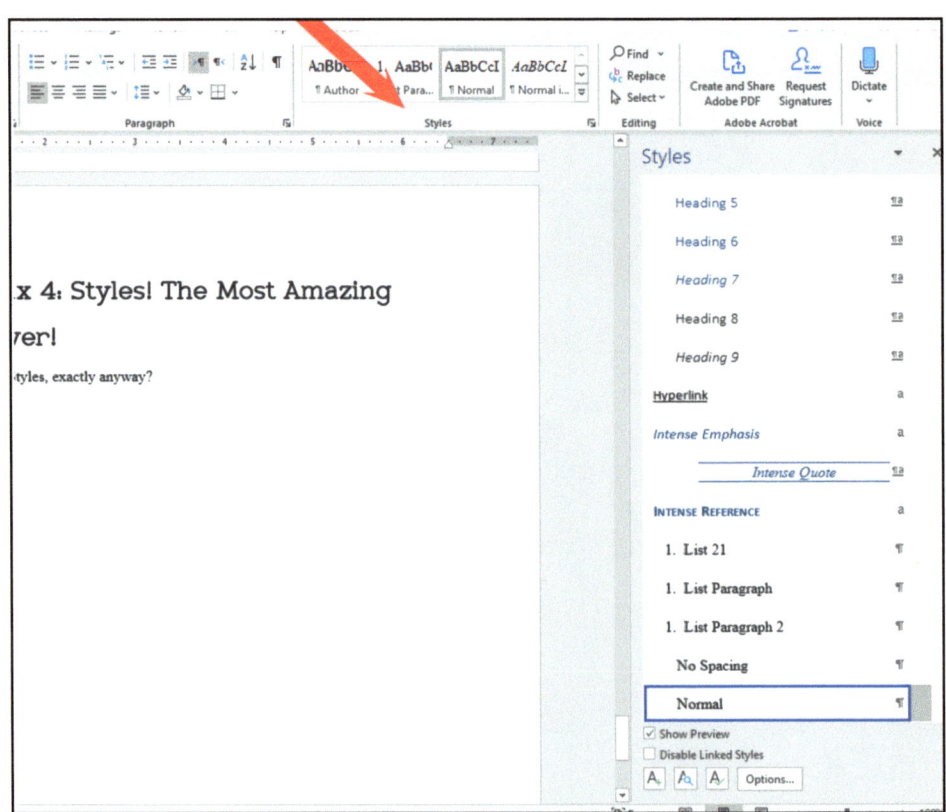

Styles are basically shortcuts for setting up Headings and body text every time we come across the next one. This is not so much something we would use a lot while writing our manuscript — do we not have enough to worry about? — but using these will help in the long run. It will most certainly help if we want to self-publish to electronic/digital format as this application demands it.

So how do they work?

Set up a heading like you want, ensuring that it is not indented, unless you want it to be, Highlight it [hold down Shift while moving the cursor to the end] then choose a "Heading" from the Styles list and placing the cursor over to the right of it where a little box with a tiny downward arrow will appear, click. Then choose the first thing in the list: Update Heading to Match Selection. Click.

Every time you type a new Heading that you want in this "style", you merely need to place your cursor (no Highlighting necessary) anywhere in the Heading you just typed and then click Heading (whatever #) and it will change what you have just typed to the Style Heading you decided to set up for this level.

The common name for text is Normal and the same steps will work for Normal.

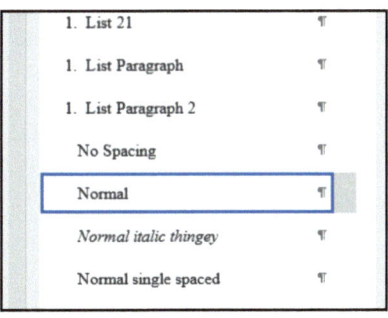
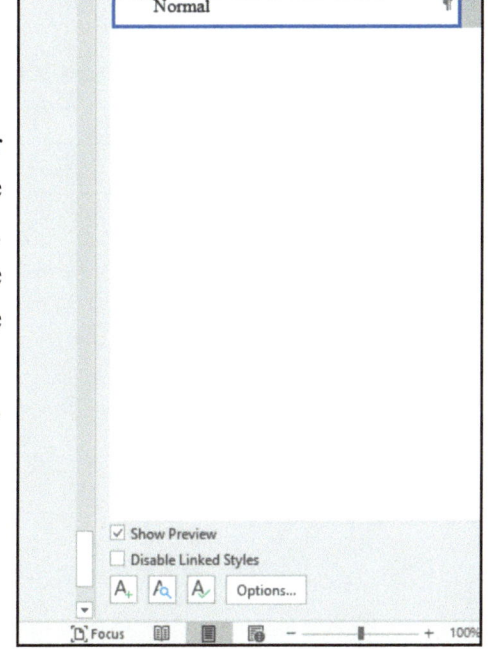

We can *add new* Styles. I usually have my Normal as regular indented text, then set up a paragraph with no indent and name that one "Normal no indent" or even, as you can see above, *Normal italic thingey*.

I don't use all these suggested Styles of course, because it slows me down trying to find them in the list. Down at the bottom you will see three boxes with As in them and a box called Options…

The first A will provide you the opportunity to create a new Style. (If there's already one in the list, it won't let you "create" another.)

The second A is the Style Inspector. I like to click on this one and then hit the little x in the upper right-hand corner and it will leave my list with only the Styles in use.

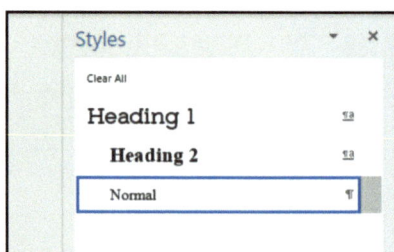

That is, <u>AS LONG AS</u> I have done a little trick in the "Options…" box. For the <u>Select styles to show</u>, I tell it In use. And for the <u>Select how list is sorted</u>, I tell it Alphabetical.)

This is the Options box. It provides two choices: (1) styles to show and (2) how list is sorted.

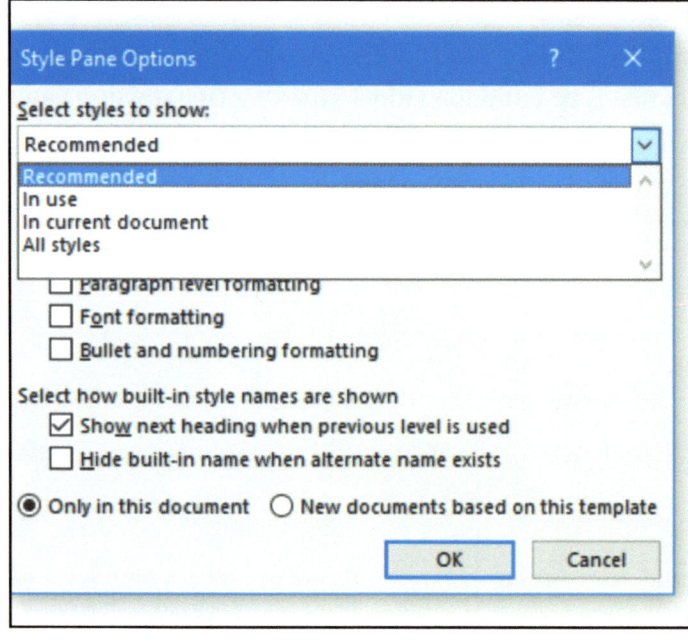

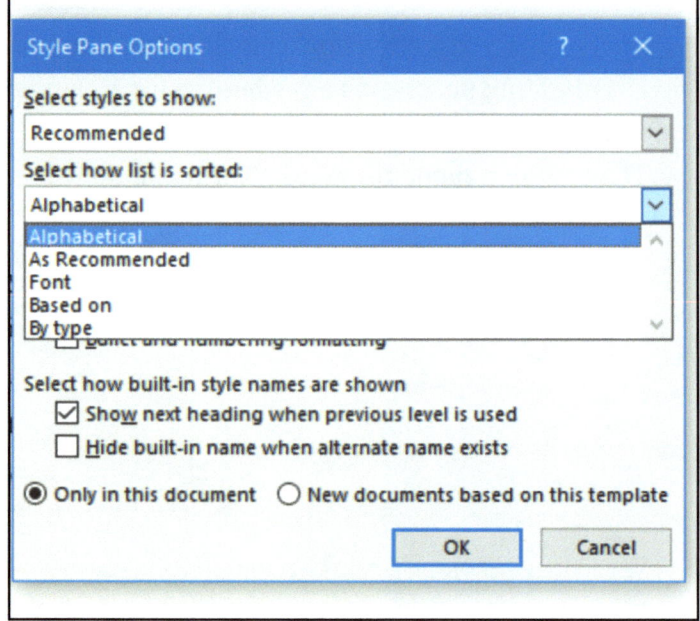

If we glance down the daunting list of Style possibilities, we can see that opportunities are there for almost anything — and this is only a small section of the list. It's almost overwhelming.

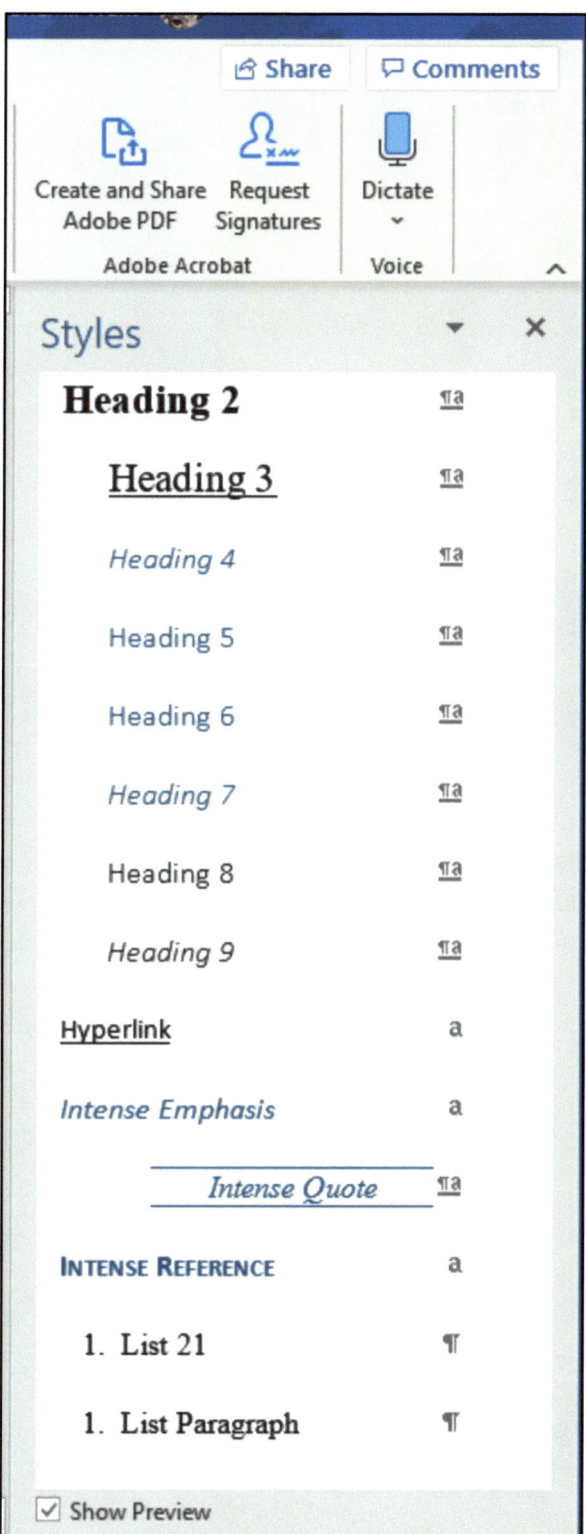

This is another application that's best played with to facilitate learning how it works. When we were little kids (at least in MY day), when we played anything at all, it was a learning opportunity bar none. Playing on a computer gives us our Internet fix and our playtime simultaneously.